THE

D0013055

THE OPEN CAGE

An
Anzia Yezierska
Collection

Selected and with an introduction by
Alice Kessler-Harris

Afterword by
Louise Levitas Henriksen

PERSEA BOOKS / NEW YORK

Fic

The selections reprinted here are by permission of Louise Levitas Henriksen.
Selections from *Hungry Hearts* are also by permission of Arno Press. Selections
were originally published as follows:

"The Miracle," from *Hungry Hearts* (Boston & New York: Houghton Mifflin, 1920) copyright renewed 1948

"America and I," from *Children of Loneliness* (New York & London: Funk & Wagnalls Co., 1923) copyright renewed 1951

"Brothers," from *Children of Loneliness* (New York & London: Funk & Wagnalls, 1923) copyright renewed 1951

"Where Lovers Dream," from *Hungry Hearts* (Boston & New York: Houghton Mifflin, 1920) copyright renewed 1948

"The Fat of the Land," from *Hungry Hearts* (Boston & New York: Houghton Mifflin, 1920 copyright renewed 1948

"The Lost 'Beautifulness'," from *Hungry Hearts* (Boston & New York: Houghton Mifflin, 1920) copyright renewed 1948

"The Lord Giveth," from *Children of Loneliness* (New York & London: Funk and Wagnalls, 1923) copyright renewed 1951

"Children of Loneliness," from *Children of Loneliness* (New York & London: Funk and Wagnalls, 1923) copyright renewed 1951

"Hester Street," from *Red Ribbon on a White Horse* (New York: Scribners, 1950) copyright renewed 1977

"Important People," from *Red Ribbon on a White Horse* (New York: Scribners, 1950) copyright renewed 1977

"My last Hollywood Script," from *Red Ribbon on a White Horse* (New York: Scribners, 1950) copyright renewed 1977

"Bread and Wine in the Wilderness," from *Red Ribbon on a White Horse* (New York: Scribners, 1950) copyright renewed 1977

"A Chair in Heaven," from *Commentary*, XXII (December, 1956) 550-557

"A Window Full of Sky," from *The Reporter*, XXXI (July, 1964) 29-31

"Take Up Your Bed and Walk," from *Chicago Jewish Forum*, XXVII (Spring, 1964).

"The Open Cage" is published here for the first time.

Introduction

Anzia Yezierska thought of herself first as a writer and then as an interpreter of the Jewish immigration experience. Her work appears to us today in the opposite posture: valuable as social history and somewhat less important for its place in literature. These stories, collected together, may reverse that image.

Yezierska was a skilled teller of tales. Gifted at the art of distilling the essence of a feeling, she could capture the poignant moment or evoke the tears of human sorrow. Instinctively, her language and form take onomatopoeic shape. The pace of a sentence matches the quickening heart beat of a tense moment. The words all but wail their despair as they catch a moment of pathos.

Her ability to write in blood, as one critic put it, was both her strength and her weakness. "She dipped her pen in her heart," they commented. Absence of form in her work—she resisted obeying what she called the textbook formula for writing—became the written equivalent of the tense and chaotic lives she saw on the Lower East Side. Yezierska relied on motion—rapid, evocative, and assertive—to carry her plots from one place to another. Her plot structures are simple, even crude, designed as vehicles for a heroine's self-discovery rather than for intrinsically interesting elements. Her characters never so much developed as they emerged: full blown archetypes of a culture and often fragments of herself. Each novel or tale works through the aspirations of the main protagonist. Success or failure matter less than self awareness. And what matters most of all is the recognition, despairing or hopeful, of the double reality of the immigrant experience. The eyes of the central figure see the world and interpret it for the reader. The dreams, like those in these stories, were her dreams, the struggle hers, and hers the success and the disillusionment of these tales.

Technique and subject both grew out of the literary realism which was then the mode. Yezierska reached literary maturity in the early 1900s. That decade offered freedom to transcend the socially acceptable, to write about the unseemly, the nether world. Theodore Dreiser, Upton Sinclair, Stephen Crane—these must have been the companions of her young twenties. But the detailed dissection of mind and matter in which these authors engaged was not Yezierska's style. As she searched, between 1910 and 1920, to come to terms with a style and a self, Yezierska seems consciously to have turned to an idiom that did not merely describe her characters, but that felt them. Alfred Kazin, speaking of Sherwood Anderson and Sinclair Lewis describes this as a realism that "no longer had to fight for its life . . . . a realism essentially instinctive," concerned with the "transcription of the average experience, with reproducing, sometimes parodying, but always participating in, experiences which make up the native culture." It is a description that exactly fits Yezierska's awareness of her need to write. In "My Own People," a tale from her first book, *Hungry Hearts* (1920), she wrote, "It's not me— it's their cries—my own people—crying in me! Hannah Breineh, Shmendrek, they will not be stilled in me, till all America stops to listen."

A Jewish immigrant community throbbed in Yiddish, and Yezierska worked at reproducing its essence. She never wrote in Yiddish, though her prose sometimes reads like a direct translation. Jo Ann Boydston has convincingly demonstrated that she could write fine English prose. But she chose to create a style in which the Yiddish idiom, translated into English, evoked the cultural context she wanted to recreate. Yezierska described the process she used to achieve this end in a lecture she gave when she was in her eighties. Speaking of the woman after whom she had modeled Hannah Breineh, protagonist of the prize-winning tale, "The Fat of the Land," she said:

> She was so full of color, but when I tried to put her down on paper, the words stared back at me stiff and wooden. But I went on writing and rewriting, possessed by the need to get at something unutterable, that could only be said in the white spaces between the words. Weeks, months, I labored over a bit of dialogue, over a fragment of a scene till the words that blocked the meaning got out of the way, and the characters leaped to life.

After she became famous, Yezierska encouraged the notion that her prose was the natural outpouring of her feeling. She had probably begun writing stories about 1912. Her first publication, "The Free Vacation House," came in 1915. Then there was a steady trickle of stories until they were collected into *Hungry Hearts*, in 1920. By the time *Hungry Hearts* had been sold to the movies, and she had become a rags-to-riches heroine, both the style and the legend were fixed. Yezierska never denied the flood of stories that described how she had written on scraps of paper, by candlelight, or, as Gertrude Atherton put it, "in a room occupied by twelve other people."

The myth was self-confirming. It reflected figuratively, if not literally, the fiery, demanding, and ambitious personna who both wrote the stories and appeared in them. Passion was part of her temperament, and much of her fame was built on the emotional power of her prose. The attention Yezierska drew for *Hungry Hearts*, and for her first novel, *Salome of the Tenements* — which led Gertrude Atherton to call her a "genius" —

could not but have encouraged Yezierska to continue in the mode she had adopted. Atherton, like many critics overlooked what she called "the crudities of such beginnings" in favor of the mastery with which Yezierska drew her Jewish characters. Like critics of the earlier book, she applauded "this flaming and burning of elemental passion." But by the time of her third book, a collection of stories called *Children of Loneliness* (1923), the unvarying style had begun to pall. William Lyons Phelps, acknowledging with awe the "core of fire" in her work, nevertheless commented, "if she would learn to command and subdue her emotions, success [would be] assured."

For a while it was. Yezierska touched something quintessential of the 1920's that transcended the narrow themes of immigrant adjustment with which her stories superficially dealt. In a decade that began with the Justice Department's deportation of aliens alleged to be threatening the overthrow of America's most cherished values, in a decade that witnessed the execution of Nicola Sacco and Bartolomeo Vanzetti for alien opinions, in a decade tortured by nativism, anti-radicalism, and racism, Yezierska offered a curiously reassuring message. She could describe her people in language redolent of Yiddish with a message hearteningly American. Her mission, as she articulated it in her tales and in her interviews, was to interpret her people to America. She would, as she says in "America and I," "build a bridge of understanding between the American-born and myself. Since their life was shut out from such as me, I began to open my life and the lives of my people to them. And life draws life. In only writing about the ghetto, I found America."

Yezierska believed in the American dream: it was part and parcel of her own ambition to "make herself for a person." It was essential to sustaining her faith in this land of immigrants. Again and again, her stories confirm her trust by acts of faith. In "The Miracle," an American-born lover appears. In "America and I," it is her faith that restores. In "The Lord Giveth," the community responds. Even in those tales, such as "The Lost 'Beautifulness,'" which end badly, Yezierska's tone is one of sorrow rather than of condemnation.

In the twenties, too, it was plausible for a young woman who dreamed of success to articulate it without seeming alien to a culture that had only recently acknowledged women's independent aspirations. The ambitious women who people her tales may have had their roots in an immigrant tradition, but they were not stifled as they might have been a generation earlier by a discouraging environment. Edith Wharton's Lilly Bart, the fine heroine of the *House of Mirth*, whose options close up around her, contrasts strangely with Yezierska's women whose fists fly in the face of a tradition that hems them in. But Fitzgerald's flappers and even Lewis' Carol Kennicott of *Main Street* would have recognized Yezierska's conviction that women could achieve success by their own efforts. Sonja of *Salome of the Tenements* abandons a rich and powerful husband—everything she had always wanted—in order to find her way alone. Yezierska wrote in the *Literary Digest* in 1923, "I saw America was a new world in the making, that anyone who has something real in him can find a way to contribute himself in this new world. But I saw I had to fight for my chance to give what I had to give, with the same life and death earnestness with which a man fights for his bread."

Ambition vied with materialism in her fiction. Although in real life she gave up money for the freedom to write, her novels were always clear about the degradation of poverty, and they systematically rejected a cold-blooded charity. She had no patience for the romantic

ix

rich who thought povety bred "closeness" nor could she stand the ministrations of charity dispensers who saw only evil in the poor. Yet, if she had been a socialist in her younger days, by the 1920s, she had other priorities. "Give me only," she wrote, "the democracy of beauty, and I'll leave the fight for government democracy to politicians and educated old maids."

In this first decade of success, Yezierska's style and message harmonized with the spirit of a period. When she achieved reknown, and when she wrote her best fiction, the Jewish Lower East Side had already reached its peak and was beginning to disintegrate. A generation of immigrants had begun to send their children off to college. They had reaped the rewards of thrift and hard work, and were slowly moving to Brooklyn, the Bronx, and Riverside Drive. Yezierska was in her element as she captured the tensions faced by the American-born and educated children and the heartbreak of parents who could not let them go. It is the theme of "Children of Loneliness," one of her best stories, and of her most praised story, "The Fat of the Land." It appears in *Bread Givers* (1925) and it reappears in *All I Could Never Be* (1932).

But as the community of immigrants slowly disintegrated and as her success moved her away from what was left of it, her material ran dry and the emotional outrage began to seem strangely out of place. She did not lose her subject, yet the form in which she wrote could no longer adequately capture the complexity of the changing community. The great depression that began in 1929 altered priorities, and clanging hollowly against the individual salvation preached by her earlier novels. *All I Could Never Be*, her last published novel of the period, captures the tension. This tale of an immigrant girl, who aspired to success and made it, was different from the others. Its plot played with a young woman who returns to the ghetto as an interpreter. In her romantic illusions about her boss, and in the role she plays in the team of researchers, Fanya Iwanovna captures the contradictions between individual success and the struggle for social justice. Fanya, like Yezierska, chose individual solutions. A message appropriate for the twenties fell with a dull thud into the thirties. Even though Yezierska had moderated her language, chosen a more structured form, and attempted to build supporting characters, the novel paid insufficient attention to plot and theme to attract much attention. Like Fanya, Yezierska gave up the emotional power that was her strength but she had not yet worked out an alternative mode.

The fiction of this period, and especially the short stories that make most effective use of her passion, were not followed by anything as powerful until the publication of her thoughtful *Red Ribbon on a White Horse* (1950). Here, in a book which is a collection of loosely woven semi-fictional vignettes, she reviewed her past, assessed the decisions she had made, and seemed to make her peace with her career aspirations. She had seen herself as a failure and a disgrace, she wrote, but suddenly the anxiety and the insecurity had receded into an acceptance of herself. "Why had I no premonition," she asked, "in the wandering years when I was hungering and thirsting for recognition, that this quiet joy, this sanctuary was waiting for me after I sank back to anonymity?" The revelation seemed to free her from old themes and in her seventies she began again to publish stories that related to her life as she was then living it.

The stories in the section called "Old Age," less well-known than the earlier fiction and never collected in book form, reflect this period. Her style had altered slightly. These stories focus somewhat less on self-involved ambition than on compassion and a demand for social justice. Yezierska relied less now on verbal outrage to make her points than on the subtle nuances of plot and structure. "The Open Cage," previously unpublished and written when she was in her eighties, was something of a breakthrough. Like the trapped bird she was first afraid of, and then did not wish to free, Yezierska would have taken wing and flown. But she was old and poor and could only speculate on the luxury of freedom.

We have come full circle and two generations away from the Lower East Side, the search for our past draws us back to Anzia Yezierska's stories. Once there, we are held by her skill at rendering character in a few sharp words—by a pen dipped in the heart. The stories collected here have a place in our historical and our literary past. From a literary perspective, they belong to the new realism of the 1920s, where they take their place in the genre of immigrant novels and autobiographies. Yezierska was not the first storyteller to interpret immigrants to America for Abraham Cahan preceded her with *Yekl, the Imported Bridegroom* and *The Rise of David Levinsky.* Nor was she the most sophisticated; Henry Roth's *Call It Sleep* must win that prize. But in evoking the joy and pain of the Jewish immigrant tradition, she has no peer. She is the precursor of a generation of Jewish immigrants whose written language is English, but who breathed and lived in Yiddish. From a historical perspective, the stories carry us back into the collective experience of a mass migration as it settled into the soul of America.

This collection of short stories and vignettes is selected to illustrate both sides of Yezierska: her craft as a storyteller and her experience as an immigrant woman. Like Anzia Yezierska, many came to America, young, full of hopeful energy. They struggled to make it and finally achieved some place, some stature, some sense of self-esteem. Then a plateau, a coming to terms with one's life, and finally old age. Yezierska selected her themes from her life. It is appropriate that any collection of stories reflect her life span. Many excellent tales have been of necessity excluded. Those that remain represent not a time but an experience. I hope that they will evoke in form as well as content, the collective consciousness of a generation.

Alice Kessler-Harris
New York
November, 1978

Contents

Introduction, by Alice Kessler-Harris   v

I. Dreams   1
The Miracle   3
America and I   20
Brothers   34
Where Lovers Dream   62

II. Struggle   75
The Fat of the Land   77
The Lost "Beautifulness"   105
The Lord Giveth   125

III. Success   143
Children of Loneliness   145
Hester Street   164
Important People   176
My Last Hollywood Script   184
Bread and Wine in the Wilderness   191

IV. Old Age   211
A Chair in Heaven   213
A Window Full of Sky   230
Take Up Your Bed and Walk   237
The Open Cage   245

Afterword about Anzia Yezierska by her daughter
Louise Levitas Henriksen   253

I

DREAMS

The Miracle

Like all people who have nothing, I lived on dreams. With nothing but my longing for love, I burned my way through stone walls till I got to America. And what happened to me when I became an American is more than I can picture before my eyes, even in a dream.

I was a poor Melamid's daughter in Savel, Poland. In my village, a girl without a dowry was a dead one. The only kind of a man that would give a look on a girl without money was a widower with a dozen children, or someone with a hump or on crutches.

There was the village water-carrier with red, teary eyes, and warts on his cracked lip. There was the janitor of the bath-house, with a squash nose, and long, black nails with all the dirt of the world under them. Maybe one of these uglinesses might yet take pity on me and do me the favor to marry me. I shivered and grew cold through all my bones at the thought of them.

Like the hunger for bread was my hunger for love. My life was nothing to me. My heart was empty. Nothing I did was real without love. I used to spend nights crying on my pillow, praying to God: "I want love! I want love! I can't live—I can't breathe without love!"

And all day long I'd ask myself: "Why was I born? What is the use of dragging on day after day, wasting myself eating, sleeping, dressing? What is the meaning of anything without love?" And my heart was so hungry I couldn't help feeling and dreaming that somehow, somewhere, there must be a lover waiting for me. But how and where could I find my lover was the one longing that burned in my heart by day and by night.

Then came the letter from Hanneh Hayyeh, Zlata's daughter, that fired me up to go to America for my lover.

"America is a lover's land," said Hanneh Hayyeh's letter. "In America millionaires fall in love with poorest girls. Matchmakers are out of style, and a girl can get herself married to a man without the worries for a dowry."

"God from the world!" began knocking my heart. "How grand to live where the kind of a man you get don't depend on how much money your father can put down! If I could only go to America! There—there waits my lover for me."

That letter made a holiday all over Savel. The butcher, the grocer, the shoemaker, everybody stopped his work and rushed to our house to hear my father read the news from the Golden Country.

"Stand out your ears to hear my great happiness," began Hanneh Hayyeh's letter. "I, Hanneh Hayyeh, will marry myself to Solomon Cohen, the boss from the shirtwaist factory, where all day I was working sewing on buttons. If you could only see how the man is melting away his heart for me! He kisses me after each step I walk. The only wish from his heart is to make me for a lady. Think only, he is buying me a piano! I should learn piano lessons as if I were from millionaires."

Fire and lightning burst through the crowd. "Hanneh Hayyeh a lady!" They nudged and winked one to the other as they looked on the loose fatness of Zlata, her mother, and saw before their eyes Hanneh Hayyeh, with her thick, red lips, and her shape so fat like a puffed-out barrel of yeast.

"In America is a law called 'ladies first,'" the letter went on. "In the cars the men must get up to give their seats to the women. The men hold the babies on their hands and carry the bundles for the women, and even help with the dishes. There are not enough women to go around in America. And the men run after the women, and not like in Poland, the women running after the men."

Gewalt! What an excitement began to burn through the whole village when they heard of Hanneh Hayyeh's luck!

The ticket agents from the ship companies seeing how Hanneh Hayyeh's letter was working like yeast in the air for America, posted up big signs by all the market fairs: "Go to America, the New World. Fifty rubles a ticket."

"Fifty rubles! Only fifty rubles! And there waits your lover!" cried my heart.

Oi weh! How I was hungering to go to America after that! By day and by night I was tearing and turning over the earth, how to get to my lover on the other side of the world.

"Nu, Zalmon?" said my mother, twisting my father around to what I wanted. "It's not so far from sense what Sara Reisel is saying. In Savel, without a dowry, she has no chance to get a man, and if we got to wait much longer she will be too old to get one anywhere."

"But from where can we get together the fifty rubles?"asked my father. "Why don't it will itself in you to give your daughter the moon?"

I could no more think on how to get the money than they. But I was so dying to go, I felt I could draw the money out from the sky.

One night I could not fall asleep. I lay in the darkness and stillness, my wild, beating heart on fire with dreams of my lover. I put out my hungry hands and prayed to my lover through the darkness: "Oh, love, love! How can I get the fifty rubles to come to you?"

In the morning I got up like one choking for air. We were sitting down to eat breakfast, but I couldn't taste nothing. I felt my head drop into my hands from weakness.

"Why don't you try to eat something?" begged my mother, going over to me.

"Eat?" I cried, jumping up like one mad. "How can I eat? How can I sleep? How can I breathe in this deadness? I want to go to America. I *must* go, and I *will* go!"

My mother began wringing her hands. "Oi weh! Mine heart! The knife is on our neck. The landlord is hollering for the unpaid rent, and it wills itself in you America?"

"Are you out of your head?" cried my father.

"What are you dreaming of golden hills on the sky? How can we get together the fifty rubles for a ticket?"

I stole a look at Yosef, my younger brother. Nothing that was sensible ever laid in his head to do; but if there was anything wild, up in the air that willed itself in him, he could break through stone walls to get it. Yosef gave a look around the house. Everything was old and poor, and not a thing to get money on—nothing except father's Saifer Torah—the Holy Scrolls—and mother's silver candlesticks, her wedding present from our grandmother.

"Why not sell the Saifer Torah and the candlesticks?" said Yosef.

Nobody but my brother would have dared to breathe such a thing.

"What? A Jew sell the Saifer Torah or the Sabbath candlesticks?" My father fixed on us his burning eyes like flaming wells. His hands tightened over his heart.

He couldn't speak. He just looked on the Saifer Torah, and then on us with a look that burned like live coals on our naked bodies. "What?" he gasped. "Should I sell my life, my soul from generation and generation? Sell my Saifer Torah? Not if the world goes under!"

There was a stillness of thunder about to break. Everybody heard everybody's heart beating.

"Did I live to see this black day?" moaned my father, choking from quick breathing. "Mine own son, mine Kaddish—mine Kaddish tells me to sell the Holy Book that our forefathers shed rivers of blood to hand down to us."

"What are you taking it so terrible?" said my brother"Doesn't it stand in the Talmud that to help marry his daughter a man may sell the holiest thing—even the Holy Book?"

"*Are there miracles in America?* Can she yet get there a man at her age and without a dowry?"

"If Hanneh Hayyeh, who is older than Sara Reisel and not half as good-looking," said my brother, "could get a boss from a factory, then whom cannot Sara Reisel pick out? And with her luck all of us will be lifted over to America."

My father did not answer. I waited, but still he did not answer.

At last I burst out with all the tears choking in me for years: "Is your old Saifer Torah that hangs on the wall dearer to you than that I should marry? The Talmud tells you to sell the holiest thing to help marry your daughter, but you—you love yourself more than your own child!"

Then I turned to my mother. I hit my hands on the table and cried in a voice that made her tremble and grow frightened: "Maybe you love your silver candlesticks more than your daughter's happiness? To whom can I marry myself here, I ask you, only—to the bath janitor, to the water-carrier? I tell you I'll kill myself if you don't help me get away! I can't stand no more this deadness here. I must get away. And you must give up everything to help me get away. All I need is a chance. I can do a million times better than Hanneh Hayyeh. I got a head. I got brains. I feel I can marry myself to the greatest man in America."

My mother stopped crying, took up the candlesticks from the mantelpiece and passed her hands over them. "It's like a piece from my flesh," she said. "We grew up with this, you children and I, and my mother and my mother's mother. This and the Saifer Torah are the only things that shine up the house for the Sabbath."

She couldn't go on, her words choked in her so. I am seeing yet how she looked, holding the candlesticks in her hands, and her eyes that she turned on us. But then I didn't see anything but to go to America.

She walked over to my father, who sat with his head in his hands, stoned with sadness. "Zalmon!" she sobbed. "The blood from under my nails I'll give away, only my child should have a chance to marry herself well. I'll give away my candlesticks—"

Even my brother Yosef's eyes filled with tears, so he quick jumped up and began to whistle and move around. "You don't have to sell them," he cried, trying to make it light in the air. "You can pawn them by Moisheh Itzek, the usurer, and as soon as Sara Reisel will get herself married, she'll send us the money to get them out again, and we'll yet live to take them over with us to America."

I never saw my father look so sad. He looked like a man from whom the life is bleeding away. "I'll not stand myself against your happiness," he said, in a still voice. "I only hope this will be to your luck and that you'll get married quick, so we could take out the Saifer Torah from the pawn."

In less than a week the Saifer Torah and the candle-sticks were pawned and the ticket bought. The whole village was ringing with the news that I am going to America. When I walked in the street people pointed on me with their fingers as if I were no more the same Sara Reisel.

Everybody asked me different questions.

"Tell me how it feels to go to America? Can you yet sleep nights like other people?"

"When you'll marry yourself in America, will you yet remember us?"

God from the world! That last Friday night before I went to America! Maybe it is the last time we are to-gether was in everybody's eyes. Everything that hap-pened seemed so different from all other times. I felt I was getting ready to tear my life out from my body.

Without the Saifer Torah the house was dark and empty. The sun, the sky, the whole heaven shined from that Holy Book on the wall, and when it was taken out it left an aching emptiness on the heart, as if something beautiful passed out of our lives.

I yet see before me my father in the Rabbi's cap, with eyes that look far away into things; the way he sang the prayer over the wine when he passed around the glass for everyone to give a sip. The tears rolled out from my little sister's eyes down her cheeks and fell into the wine. On that my mother, who was all the time wiping her tears, burst out crying. "Shah! Shah!" commanded my father, rising up from his chair and beginning to walk around the room. "It's Sabbath night, when every Jew should be happy. Is this the way you give honor to God on His one day that He set aside for you?"

On the next day, that was Sabbath, father as if held us up in his hands, and everybody behaved himself. A stranger coming in couldn't see anything that was going on, except that we walked so still and each one by himself, as if somebody dying was in the air over us.

On the going-away morning, everybody was around our house waiting to take me to the station. Everybody wanted to give a help with the bundles. The moving along to the station was like a funeral. Nobody could hold in their feelings any longer. Everybody fell on my neck to kiss me, as if it was my last day on earth.

"Remember you come from Jews. Remember to pray every day," said my father, putting his hands over my head, like in blessing on the day of Atonement.

"Only try that we should be together soon again," were the last words from my mother as she wiped her eyes with the corner of her shawl.

"Only don't forget that I want to study, and send for me as quick as you marry yourself," said Yosef, smiling good-bye with tears in his eyes.

As I saw the train coming, what wouldn't I have given to stay back with the people in Savel forever! I wanted to cry out: "Take only away my ticket! I don't want any more America! I don't want any more my lover!"

But as soon as I got into the train, although my eyes were still looking back to the left-behind faces, and my ears were yet hearing the good-byes and the partings, the thoughts of America began stealing into my heart. I was thinking how soon I'd have my lover and be rich like Hanneh Hayyeh. And with my luck, everybody was going to be happy in Savel. The dead people will stop dying and all the sorrows and troubles of the world will be wiped away with my happiness.

I didn't see the day. I didn't see the night. I didn't see the ocean. I didn't see the sky. I only saw my lover in America, coming nearer and nearer to me, till I could feel his eyes bending on me so near that I got frightened and began to tremble. My heart ached so with the joy of his nearness that I quick drew back and turned away, and began to talk to the people that were pushing and crowding themselves on the deck.

Nu, I got to America.

Ten hours I pushed a machine in a shirtwaist factory, when I was yet lucky to get work. And always my head was drying up with saving and pinching and worrying to send home a little from the little I earned. All that my face saw all day long was girls and machines—and nothing else. And even when I came already home from work, I could only talk to the girls in the working girls' boarding house, or shut myself up in my dark, lonesome bedroom. No family, no friends, nobody to get me acquainted with nobody! The only men I saw were what passed me by in the street and in cars.

"Is this 'lovers' land'?" was calling in my heart. "Where are my dreams that were so real to me in the old country?"

Often in the middle of the work I felt like stopping all the machines and crying out to the world the heaviness that pressed on my heart. Sometimes when I walked in the street I felt like going over to the first man I met and cry out to him: "Oh, I'm so lonely! I'm so lonely!"

One day I read in the Jewish "Tageblatt" the advertisement from Zaretzky, the matchmaker. "What harm is it if I try my luck?" I said to myself. "I can't die away an old maid. Too much love burns in my heart to stand back like a stone and only see how other people are happy. I want to tear myself out from my deadness. I'm in a living grave. I've got to lift myself up. I have nobody to try for me, and maybe the matchmaker will help."

As I walked up Delancey Street to Mr. Zaretzky, the street was turning with me. I didn't see the crowds. I didn't see the pushcart peddlers with their bargains. I didn't hear the noises or anything. My eyes were on the sky, praying: "Gottuniu! Send me only the little bit of luck!"

"Nu? Nu? What need you?" asked Mr. Zaretzky when I entered.

I got red with shame in the face the way he looked at me. I turned up my head. I was too proud to tell him for what I came. Before I walked in I thought to tell him everything. But when I looked on his face and saw his hard eyes, I couldn't say a word. I stood like a yok unable to move my tongue. I went to the matchmaker with my heart, and I saw before me a stone. The stone was talking to me—but—but—he was a stone!

"Are you looking for a shidduch?" he asked.

"Yes," I said, proud, but crushed.

"You know I charge five dollars for the stepping in," he bargained.

It got cold by my heart. It wasn't only to give him the five dollars, nearly a whole week's wages, but his thick-skinness for being only after the money. But I couldn't help myself—I was like in his fists hypnotized. And I gave him the five dollars.

I let myself go to the door, but he called me back.

"Wait, wait. Come in and sit down. I didn't question you yet."

"About what?"

"I got to know how much money you got saved before I can introduce you to anybody."

"Oh—h—h! Is it only depending on the *money?*"

"Certainly. No move in this world without money," he said, taking a pinch of snuff in his black, hairy fingers and sniffing it up in his nose.

I glanced on his thick neck and greasy, red face. "And to him people come looking for love," I said to myself, shuddering. Oh, how it burned in my heart, but still I went on, "Can't I get a man in America without money?"

He gave a look on me with his sharp yes. Gottuniu! What a look! I thought I was sinking into the floor.

"There are plenty of *young* girls with money that are begging themselves the men to take them. So what can you expect? *Not young, not lively, and without money, too?* But, anyhow, I'll see what I can do for you."

He took out a little book from his vest-pocket and looked through the names.

"What trade do you got on your hands?" he asked, turning to me. "Sometimes a dressmaker or a hair-dresser that can help make a living for a man, maybe—"

I couldn't hear any more. It got black before my eyes, my voice stopped inside of me.

"If you want to listen to sense from a friend, so I have a good match for you," he said, following me to the door. "I have on my list a widower with not more than five or six children. He has a grand business, a herring-stand on Hester Street. He don't ask for no money, and he don't make an objection if the girl is in years, so long as she knows how to cook well for him."

How I got myself back to my room I don't know. But for two days and for two nights I lay still on my bed, unable to move. I looked around on my empty walls, thinking, thinking, "Where am I? Is this the world? Is this America?"

Suddenly I sprang up from bed. "What can come from pitying yourself?" I cried. "If the world kicks you down and makes nothing of you, you bounce yourself up and make something of yourself." A fire blazed up in me to rise over the world because I was downed by the world.

"Make a person of yourself," I said. "Begin to learn English. Make yourself for an American if you want to live in America. American girls don't go to match-makers. American girls don't run after a man: if they don't get a husband they don't think the world is over; they turn their mind to something else.

"Wake up!" I said to myself. "You want love to come to you? Why don't you give it out to other people? Love the women and children, everybody in the street and the shop. Love the rag-picker and the drunkard, the bad and the ugly. All those whom the world kicks down you pick up and press to your heart with love."

As I said this I felt wells of love that choked in me all my life flowing out of me and over me. A strange, wonderful light like a lover's smile melted over me, and the sweetness of lover's arms stole around me.

The first night I went to school I felt like falling on everybody's neck and kissing them. I felt like kissing the books and the benches. It was such great happiness to learn to read and write the English words.

Because I started a few weeks after the beginning of the term, my teacher said I might stay after the class to help me catch up with my back lessons. The minute I looked on him I felt that grand feeling: "Here is a person! Here is America!" His face just shined with high thoughts. There was such a beautiful light in his eyes that it warmed my heart to steal a look on him.

At first, when it came my turn to say something in the class, I got so excited the words stuck and twisted in my mouth and I couldn't give out my thoughts. But the teacher didn't see my nervousness. He only saw that I had something to say, and he helped me say it. How or what he did I don't know. I only felt his look of understanding flowing into me like draughts of air to one who is choking.

Long after I already felt free and easy to talk to him alone after the class, I looked at all the books on his desk. "Oi weh!" I said to him, "if I only knew half of what is in your books, I couldn't any more sit still in the chair like you. I'd fly in the air with the joy of so much knowledge."

"Why are you so eager for learning?" he asked me.

"Because I want to make a person of myself," I answered. "Since I got to work for low wages and I can't be young any more, I'm burning to get among people where it's not against a girl if she is in years and without money."

His hand went out to me. "I'll help you," he said. "But you must first learn to get hold of yourself."

Such a beautiful kindness went out of his heart to me with his words! His voice, and the goodness that shone from his eyes, made me want to burst out crying, but I choked back my tears till I got home. And all night long I wept on my pillow: "Fool! What is the matter with you? Why are you crying?" But I said, "I can't help it. He is so beautiful!"

My teacher was so much above me that he wasn't a man to me at all. He was a God. His face lighted up the shop for me, and his voice sang itself in me everywhere I went. It was like healing medicine to the flaming fever within me to listen to his voice. And then I'd repeat to myself his words and live in them as if they were religion.

Often as I sat at the machine sewing the waists I'd forget what I was doing. I'd find myself dreaming in the air. "Ach!" I asked myself, "what was that beautifulness

in his eyes that made the lowest nobody feel like a somebody? What was that about him that when his smile fell
on me I felt lifted up to the sky away from all the coldness and the ugliness of the world? Gottunui!" I prayed,
"if I could only always hold on to the light of high
thoughts that shined from him. If I could only always
hear in my heart the sound of his voice I would need
nothing more in life. I would be happier than a bird in the
air.

"Friend," I said to him once, "if you could but teach
me how to get cold in the heart and clear in the head like
you are!"

He only smiled at me and looked far away. His calmness was like the sureness of money in the bank. Then
he turned and looked on me, and said: "I am not so cold in
the heart and clear in the head as I make-believe. I am
bound. I am a prisoner of convention."

"You make-believe—you bound?" I burst out. "You
who do not have foreladies or bosses—you who do not
have to sell yourself for wages—you who only work for
love and truth—you a prisoner?"

"True, I do not have bosses just as you do," he said.
"But still I am not free. I am bound by formal education
and conventional traditions. Though you work in a
shop, you are really freer than I. You are not repressed
as I am by the fear and shame of feeling. You could teach
me more than I could teach you. You could teach me how
to be natural."

"I'm not so natural like you think," I said. "I'm afraid."

He smiled at me out of his eyes. "What are you
afraid of?"

"I'm afraid of my heart," I said, trying to hold back
the blood rushing to my face. "I'm burning to get calm
and sensible like the born Americans. But how can I help

it? My heart flies away from me like a wild bird. How can I learn to keep myself down on earth like the born Amerians?"

"But I don't want you to get down on earth like the Americans. That is just the beauty and the wonder of you. We Americans are too much on earth; we need more of your power to fly. If you would only know how much you can teach us Americans. You are the promise of the centuries to come. You are the heart, the creative pulse of America to be."

I walked home on wings. My teacher said that I could help him; that I had something to give to Americans. "But how could I teach him?" I wondered; "I who had never had a chance to learn anything except what he taught me. And what had I to give to the Americans, I who am nothing but dreams and longings and hunger for love?"

When school closed down for vacation, it seemed to me all life stopped in the world. I had no more class to look forward to, no more chance of seeing my teacher. As I faced the emptiness of my long vacation, all the light went out of my eyes, and all the strength out of my arms and fingers.

For nearly a week I was like without air. There was no school. One night I came home from the shop and threw myself down on the bed. I wanted to cry, to let out the heavy weight that pressed on my heart, but I couldn't cry. My tears felt like hot, burning sand in my eyes.

"Oi-i-i! I can't stand it no more, this emptiness," I groaned. "Why don't I kill myself? Why don't something happen to me? No consumption, no fever, no plague or death ever comes to save me from this terrible world. I have to go on suffering and choking inside myself till I grow mad."

I jumped up from the bed, threw open the window, and began fighting with the deaf-and-dumb air in the air-shaft.

"What is the matter with you?" I cried. "You are going out of your head. You are sinking back into the old ways from which you dragged yourself out with your studies. Studies! What did I get from all my studies? Nothing. Nothing. I am still in the same shop with the same shirtwaists. A lot my teacher cares for me once the class is over."

A fire burned up in me that he was already forgetting me. And I shot out a letter to him:

"You call yourself a teacher? A friend? How can you go off in the country and drop me out of your heart and out of your head like a readover book you left on the shelf of your shut-down classroom? How can you enjoy your vacation in the country while I'm in the sweatshop? You learned me nothing. You only broke my heart. What good are all the books you ever gave me? They don't tell me how to be happy in a factory. They don't tell me how to keep alive in emptiness, or how to find something beautiful in the dirt and ugliness in which I got to waste away. I want life. I want people. I can't live inside my head as you do."

I sent the letter off in the madness in which I wrote it, without stopping to think; but the minute after I dropped it in the mail-box my reason came again to my head. I went back tearing my hair. "What have I done? Meshugeneh!"

Walking up the stairs I saw my door open. I went in. The sky is falling to the earth! Am I dreaming? There was my teacher sitting on my trunk! My teacher come to see me? Me, in my dingy room? For a minute it got blind before my eyes, and I didn't know where I was any more.

"I had to come," he said, the light of heaven shining on me out of his eyes. "I was so desolate without you. I tried to say something to you before I left for my vacation, but the words wouldn't come. Since I have been away I have written you many letters, but I did not mail them, for they were like my old self from which I want to break away."

He put his cool, strong hand into mine. "You can save me," he said. "You can free me from the bondage of age-long repressions. You can lift me out of the dead grooves of sterile intellectuality. Without you I am the dry dust of hopes unrealized. You are fire and sunshine and desire. You make life changeable and beautiful and full of daily wonder."

I couldn't speak. I was so on fire with his words. Then, like whirlwinds in my brain, rushed out the burning words of the matchmaker: "Not young, not lively, and without money, too!"

"You are younger than youth," he said, kissing my hands. "Every day of your unlived youth shall be relived with love, but such a love as youth could never know."

And then how it happened I don't know; but his arms were around me. "Sara Reisel, tell me, do you love me," he said, kissing me on my hair and on my eyes and on my lips.

I could only weep and tremble with joy at his touch. "The miracle!" cried my heart; "the miracle of America come true!"

America and I

As one of the dumb, voiceless ones I speak. One of the millions of immigrants beating, beating out their hearts at your gates for a breath of understanding.

Ach! America! From the other end of the earth from where I came, America was a land of living hope, woven of dreams, aflame with longing and desire.

Choked for ages in the airless oppression of Russia, the Promised Land rose up—wings for my stifled spirit —sunlight burning through my darkness—freedom singing to me in my prison—deathless songs tuning prison-bars into strings of a beautiful violin.

I arrived in America. My young, strong body, my heart and soul pregnant with the unlived lives of generations clamoring for expression.

What my mother and father and their mother and father never had a chance to give out in Russia, I would give out in America. The hidden sap of centuries would find release; colors that never saw light—songs that died unvoiced—romance that never had a chance to blossom in the black life of the Old World.

In the golden land of flowing opportunity I was to find my work that was denied me in the sterile village of my forefathers. Here I was to be free from the dead drudgery for bread that held me down in Russia. For the first time in America, I'd cease to be a slave of the belly. I'd be a creator, a giver, a human being! My work would be the living joy of fullest self-expression.

But from my high visions, my golden hopes, I had to put my feet down on earth. I had to have food and shelter. I had to have the money to pay for it.

I was in America, among the Americans, but not of them. No speech, no common language, no way to win a smile of understanding from them, only my young, strong body and my untried faith. Only my eager, empty hands, and my full heart shining from my eyes!

God from the world! Here I was with so much richness in me, but my mind was not wanted without the language. And my body, unskilled, untrained, was not even wanted in the factory. Only one of two chances was left open to me: the kitchen, or minding babies.

My first job was as a servant in an Americanized family. Once, long ago, they came from the same village from where I came. But they were so well-dressed, so well-fed, so successful in America, that they were ashamed to remember their mother tongue.

"What were to be my wages?" I ventured timidly, as I looked up to the well-fed, well-dressed "American" man and woman.

They looked at me with a sudden coldness. What have I said to draw away from me their warmth? Was it so low from me to talk of wages? I shrank back into myself like a low-down bargainer. Maybe they're so high up in well-being they can't any more understand my low thoughts for money.

From his rich height the man preached down to me that I must not be so grabbing for wages. Only just landed from the ship and already thinking about money when I should be thankful to associate with "Americans."

The woman, out of her smooth, smiling fatness assured me that this was my chance for a summer vacation in the country with her two lovely children. My great chance to learn to be a civilized being, to become an American by living with them.

So, made to feel that I was in the hands of American

friends, invited to share with them their home, their plenty, their happiness, I pushed out from my head the worry for wages. Here was my first chance to begin my life in the sunshine, after my long darkness. My laugh was all over my face as I said to them: "I'll trust myself to you. What I'm worth you'll give me." And I entered their house like a child by the hand.

The best of me I gave them. Their house cares were my house cares. I got up early. I worked till late. All that my soul hungered to give I put into the passion with which I scrubbed floors, scoured pots, and washed clothes. I was so grateful to mingle with the American people, to hear the music of the American language, that I never knew tiredness.

There was such a freshness in my brains and such a willingness in my heart that I could go on and on—not only with the work of the house, but work with my head — learning new words from the children, the grocer, the butcher, the iceman. I was not even afraid to ask for words from the policeman on the street. And every new word made me see new American things with American eyes. I felt like a Columbus, finding new worlds through every new word.

But words alone were only for the inside of me. The outside of me still branded me for a steerage immigrant. I had to have clothes to forget myself that I'm a stranger yet. And so I had to have money to buy these clothes.

The month was up. I was so happy! Now I'd have money. *My own, earned* money. Money to buy a new shirt on my back—shoes on my feet. Maybe yet an American dress and hat!

Ach! How high rose my dreams! How plainly I saw all that I would do with my visionary wages shining like a light over my head!

In my imagination I already walked in my new

American clothes. How beautiful I looked as I saw myself like a picture before my eyes! I saw how I would throw away my immigrant rags tied up in my immigrant shawl. With money to buy—free money in my hands—I'd show them that I could look like an American in a day.

Like a prisoner in his last night in prison, counting the seconds that will free him from his chains, I trembled breathlessly for the minute I'd get the wages in my hand.

Before dawn I rose.

I shined up the house like a jewel-box.

I prepared breakfast and waited with my heart in my mouth for my lady and gentleman to rise. At last I heard them stirring. My eyes were jumping out of my head to them when I saw them coming in and seating themselves by the table.

Like a hungry cat rubbing up to its boss for meat, so I edged and simpered around them as I passed them the food. Without my will, like a beggar, my hand reached out to them.

The breakfast was over. And no word yet from my wages.

"*Gottuniu!*" I thought to myself. "Maybe they're so busy with their own things they forgot it's the day for my wages. Could they who have everything know what I was to do with my first American dollars? How could they, soaking in plenty, how could they feel the longing and the fierce hunger in me, pressing up through each visionary dollar? How could they know the gnawing ache of my avid fingers for the feel of my own, earned dollars? *My* dollars that I could spend like a free person. *My* dollars that would make me feel with everybody alike!

Lunch came. Lunch past.

Oi-i weh! Not a word yet about my money.

It was near dinner. And not a word yet about my wages.

I began to set the table. But my head—it swam away from me. I broke a glass. The silver dropped from my nervous fingers. I couldn't stand it any longer. I dropped everything and rushed over to my American lady and gentleman.

"*Oi weh!* The money—my money—my wages!" I cried breathlessly.

Four cold eyes turned on me.

"Wages? Money? The four eyes turned into hard stone as they looked me up and down. "Haven't you a comfortable bed to sleep, and three good meals a day? You're only a month here. Just came to America. And you already think about money. Wait till you're worth any money. What use are you without knowing English? You should be glad we keep you here. It's like a vacation for you. Other girls pay money yet to be in the country."

It went black for my eyes. I was so choked no words came to my lips. Even the tears went dry in my throat.

I left. Not a dollar for all my work.

For a long, long time my heart ached and ached like a sore wound. If murderers would have robbed me and killed me it wouldn't have hurt me so much. I couldn't think through my pain. The minute I'd see before me how they looked at me, the words they said to me— then everything began to bleed in me. And I was helpless.

For a long, long time the thought of ever working in an "American" family made me tremble with fear, like the fear of wild wolves. No—never again would I trust myself to an "American" family, no matter how fine their language and how sweet their smile.

It was blotted out in me all trust in friendship from "Americans." But the life in me still burned to live. The hope in me still craved to hope. In darkness, in dirt, in hunger and want, but only to live on!

There had been no end to my day—working for the "American" family.

Now rejecting false friendships from higher-ups in America, I turned back to the Ghetto. I worked on a hard bench with my own kind on either side of me. I knew before I began what my wages were to be. I knew what my hours were to be. And I knew the feeling of the end of the day.

From the outside my second job seemed worse than the first. It was in a sweatshop of a Delancey Street basement, kept up by an old, wrinkled woman that looked like a black witch of greed. My work was sewing on buttons. While the morning was still dark I walked into a dark basement. And darkness met me when I turned out of the basement.

Day after day, week after week, all the contact I got with America was handling dead buttons. The money I earned was hardly enough to pay for bread and rent. I didn't have a room to myself. I didn't even have a bed. I slept on a mattress on the floor in a rat-hole of a room occupied by a dozen other immigrants. I was always hungry—oh, so hungry! The scant meals I could afford only sharpened my appetite for real food. But I felt myself better off than working in the "American" family, where I had three good meals a day and a bed to myself. With all the hunger and darkness of the sweat-shop, I had at least the evening to myself. And all night was mine. When all were asleep, I used to creep up on the roof of the tenement and talk out my heart in silence to the stars in the sky.

"Who am I? What am I? What do I want with my

life? Where is America? Is there an America? What is this wilderness in which I'm lost?"

I'd hurl my questions and then think and think. And I could not tear it out of me, the feeling that America must be somewhere, somehow—only I couldn't find it —*my America,* where I would work for love and not for a living. I was like a thing following blindly after something far off in the dark!

"Oi weh!" I'd stretch out my hand up in the air. "My head is so lost in America! What's the use of all my working if I'm not in it? Dead buttons is not me."

Then the busy season started in the shop. The mounds of buttons grew and grew. The long day stretched out longer. I had to begin with the buttons earlier and stay with them till later in the night. The old witch turned into a huge greedy maw for wanting more and more buttons.

For a glass of tea, for a slice of herring over black bread, she would buy us up to stay another and another hour, till there seemed no end to her demands.

One day, the light of self-assertion broke into my cellar darkness.

"I don't want the tea. I don't want your herring," I said with terrible boldness. "I only want to go home. I only want the evening to myself!"

"You fresh mouth, you!" cried the old witch. "You learned already too much in America. I want no clock-watchers in my shop. Out you go!"

I was driven out to cold and hunger. I could no longer pay for my mattress on the floor. I no longer could buy the bite in my mouth. I walked the streets. I knew what it is to be alone in a strange city, among strangers.

But I laughed through my tears. So I learned too much already in America because I wanted the whole evening to myself? Well America has yet to teach me still more: how to get not only the whole evening to myself, but a whole day a week like the American workers.

That sweat-shop was a bitter memory but a good school. It fitted me for a regular factory. I could walk in boldly and say I could work at something, even if it was only sewing on buttons.

Gradually, I became a trained worker. I worked in a light, airy factory, only eight hours a day. My boss was no longer a sweater and a blood-squeezer. The first freshness of the morning was mine. And the whole evening was mine. All day Sunday was mine.

Now I had better food to eat. I slept on a better bed. Now, I even looked dressed up like the American-born. But inside of me I knew that I was not yet an American. I choked with longing when I met an American-born, and I could say nothing.

Something cried dumb in me. I couldn't help it. I didn't know what it was I wanted. I only knew I wanted. I wanted. Like the hunger in the heart that never gets food.

An English class for foreigners started in our factory. The teacher had such a good, friendly face, her eyes looked so understanding, as if she could see right into my heart. So I went to her one day for an advice:

"I don't know what is with me the matter," I began. "I have no rest in me. I never yet done what I want."

"What is it you want to do, child?" she asked me.

"I want to do something with my head, my feelings. All day long, only with my hands I work."

"First you must learn English." She patted me as if I was not yet grown up. "Put your mind on that, and then we'll see."

So for a time I learned the language. I could almost begin to think with English words in my head. But in my heart the emptiness still hurt. I burned to give, to give something, to do something, to be something. The dead work with my hands was killing me. My work left only hard stones on my heart.

Again I went to our factory teacher and cried out to her: "I know already to read and write the English language, but I can't put it into words what I want. What is it in me so different that can't come out?"

She smiled at me down from her calmness as if I were a little bit out of my head. "What *do you want* to do?"

"I feel. I see. I hear. And I want to think it out. But I'm like dumb in me. I only feel I'm different—different from everybody."

She looked at me close and said nothing for a minute. "You ought to join one of the social clubs of the Women's Association," she advised.

"What's the Women's Association?" I implored greedily.

"A group of American women who are trying to help the working-girl find herself. They have a special department for immigrant girls like you."

I joined the Women's Association. On my first evening there they announced a lecture: "The Happy Worker and His Work," by the Welfare director of the United Mills Corporation.

"Is there such a thing as a happy worker at his work?" I wondered. "Happiness is only by working at what you love. And what poor girl can ever find it to work at what she loves? My old dreams about my America rushed through my mind. Once I thought that in America everybody works for love. Nobody has to worry for a living. Maybe this welfare man came to show me the *real* America that till now I sought in vain.

With a lot of polite words the head lady of the Wommen's Association introduced a higher-up that looked like the king of kings of business. Never before in my life did I ever see a man with such a sureness in his step, such power in his face, such friendly positiveness in his eye as when he smiled upon us.

"Efficiency is the new religion of business," he began. "In big business houses, even in up-to-date factories, they no longer take the first comer and give him any job that happens to stand empty. Efficiency begins at the employment office. Experts are hired for the one purpose, to find out how best to fit the worker to his work: It's economy for the boss to make the worker happy." And then he talked a lot more on efficiency in educated language that was over my head.

I didn't know exactly what it meant—efficiency—but if it was to make the worker happy at his work, then that's what I had been looking for since I came to America. I only felt from watching him that he was happy by his job. And as I looked on this clean, well-dressed, successful one, who wasn't ashamed to say he rose from an office-boy, it made me feel that I, too, could lift myself up for a person.

He finished his lecture, telling us about the Vocational-Guidance Center that the Women's Association started.

The very next evening I was at the Vocational-Guidance Center. There I found a young, college-looking woman. Smartness and health shining from her eyes! She, too, looked as if she knew her way in America. I could tell at the first glance: here is a person that is happy by what she does.

"I feel you'll understand me," I said right away.

She leaned over with pleasure in her face: "I hope I can."

"I want to work by what's in me. Only, I don't know what's in me. I only feel I'm different."

She gave me a quick, puzzled look from the corner of her eyes. "What are you doing now?"

"I'm the quickest shirtwaist hand on the floor. But my heart wastes away by such work. I think and think, and my thoughts can't come out."

"Why don't you think out your thoughts in shirt-waists? You could learn to be a designer. Earn more money."

"I don't want to look on waists. If my hands are sick from waists, how could my head learn to put beauty into them?"

"But you must earn your living at what you know, and rise slowly from job to job."

I looked at her office sign: "Vocational Guidance." "What's your vocational guidance?" I asked. "How to rise from job to job—how to earn more money?"

The smile went out from her eyes. But she tried to be kind yet. "What *do* you want?" she asked, with a sigh of last patience.

"I want America to want me."

She fell back in her chair, thunderstruck with my boldness. But yet, in a low voice of educated self-control, she tried to reason with me:

"You have to *show* that you have something special for America before America has need of you."

"But I never had a chance to find out what's in me, because I always had to work for a living. Only, I feel it's efficiency for America to find out what's in me so different, so I could give it out by my work."

Her eyes half closed as they bored through me. Her

mouth opened to speak, but no words came from her lips. So I flamed up with all that was choking in me like a house on fire:

"America gives free bread and rent to criminals in prison. They got grand houses with sunshine, fresh air, doctors and teachers, even for the crazy ones. Why don't they have free boarding-schools for immigrants—strong people—willing people? Here you see us burning up with something different, and America turns her head away from us."

Her brows lifted and dropped down. She shrugged her shoulders away from me with the look of pity we give to cripples and hopeless lunatics.

"America is no Utopia. First you must become efficient in earning a living before you can indulge in your poetic dreams."

I went away from the vocational-guidance office with all the air out of my lungs. All the light out of my eyes. My feet dragged after me like dead wood.

Till now there had always lingered a rosy veil of hope over my emptiness, a hope that a miracle would happen. I would open up my eyes some day and suddenly find the America of my dreams. As a young girl hungry for love sees always before her eyes the picture of lover's arms around her, so I saw always in my heart the vision of Utopian America.

But now I felt that the America of my dreams never was and never could be. Reality had hit me on the head as with a club. I felt that the America that I sought was nothing but a shadow—an echo—a chimera of lunatics and crazy immigrants.

Stripped of all illusion, I looked about me. The long desert of wasting days of drudgery stared me in the face. The drudgery that I had lived through, and the endless drudgery still ahead of me rose over me like a withering wilderness of sand. In vain were all my cryings, in vain were all frantic efforts of my spirit to find the living waters of understanding for my perishing lips. Sand, sand was everywhere. With every seeking, every reaching out I only lost myself deeper and deeper in a vast sea of sand.

I knew now the American language. And I knew now, if I talked to the Americans from morning till night, they could not understand what the Russian soul of me wanted. They could not understand *me* any more than if I talked to them in Chinese. Between my soul and the American soul were worlds of difference that no words could bridge over. What was that difference? What made the Americans so far apart from me?

I began to read the American history. I found from the first pages that America started with a band of Courageous Pilgrims. They had left their native country as I had left mine. They had crossed an unknown ocean and landed in an unknown country, as I.

But the great difference between the first Pilgrims and me was that they expected to make America, build America, create their own world of liberty. I wanted to find it ready made.

I read on. I delved deeper down into the American history. I saw how the Pilgrim Fathers came to a rocky desert country, surrounded by Indian savages on all sides. But undaunted, they pressed on—through danger—through famine, pestilence, and want—they pressed on. They did not ask the Indians for sympathy, for understanding. They made no demands on anybody, but on their own indomitable spirit of persistence.

And I—I was forever begging a crumb of sympathy, a gleam of understanding from strangers who could not understand.

I, when I encountered a few savage Indian scalpers, like the old witch of the sweat-shop, like my "Americanized" countryman, who cheated me of my wages— I, when I found myself on the lonely, untrodden path through which all seekers of the new world must pass, I lost heart and said: "There is no America!"

Then came a light—a great revelation! I saw America—a big idea—a deathless hope—a world still in the making. I saw that it was the glory of America that it was not yet finished. And I, the last comer, had her share to give, small or great, to the making of America, like those Pilgrims who came in the *Mayflower*.

Fired up by this revealing light, I began to build a bridge of understanding between the American-born and myself. Since their life was shut out from such as me, I began to open up my life and the lives of my people to them. And life draws life. In only writing about the Ghetto I found America.

Great chances have come to me. But in my heart is always a deep sadness. I feel like a man who is sitting down to a secret table of plenty, while his near ones and dear ones are perishing before his eyes. My very joy in doing the work I love hurts me like secret guilt, because all about me I see so many with my longings, my burning eagerness, to do and to be, wasting their days in drudgery they hate, merely to buy bread and pay rent. And America is losing all that richness of the soul.

The Americans of tomorrow, the America that is every day nearer coming to be, will be too wise, too open-hearted, too friendly-handed, to let the least last-comer at their gates knock in vain with his gifts unwanted.

Brothers

I had just begun to unpack and arrange my things in my new quarters when Hanneh Breineh edged herself confidingly into my room and started to tell me the next chapter in the history of all her roomers.

"And this last one what sleeps in the kitchen," she finished, "he's such a stingy—Moisheh the Schnorrer they call him. He washes himself his own shirts and sews together the holes from his socks to save a penny. Think only! He cooks himself his own meat once a week for the Sabbath and the rest of the time it's cabbage and potatoes or bread and herring. And the herring what he buys are the squashed and smashed ones from the bottom of the barrel. And the bread he gets is so old and hard he's got to break it with a hammer. For why should such a stingy grouch live in this world if he don't allow himself the bite in the mouth?"

It was no surprize to me that Hanneh Breineh knew all this, for everybody in her household cooked and washed in the same kitchen, and everybody knew what everybody else ate and what everybody else wore down to the number of patches on their underwear.

"And by what do you work for a living?" she asked, as she settled herself on my cot.

"I study at college by day and I give English lessons and write letters for the people in the evening."

"Ach! So you are learning for a *teacherin?*" She rose, and looked at me up and down and down and up, her red-lidded eyes big with awe. "So that's why you wanted so particular a room to yourself? Nobody in my house has a room by herself alone just like you. They all got

34

to squeeze themselves together to make it come out cheaper."

By the evening everybody in that house knew that I was a *teacherin,* and Moisheh the Schnorrer was among my first applicants for instruction.

"How much will you charge me for learning me English, a lesson?" he blurted, abrupt because of his painful bashfulness.

I looked up at the tall, ungainly creature with round, stooping shoulders, and massive, shaggy head—physically a veritable giant, yet so timid, so diffident, afraid almost of his own shadow.

"I wanna learn how to sign myself my name," he went on. "Only—you'll make it for me a little cheaper— yes?"

"Fifty cents an hour." I answered, drawn by the dumb, hunted look that cried to me out of his eyes.

Moisheh scratched his shaggy head and bit the nails of his huge, toil-worn hand. "Maybe—could you yet— perhaps—make it a little cheaper?" he fumbled.

"Aren't you working?"

His furrowed face colored with confusion. "Yes— but—but my family. I got to save myself together a penny to a penny for them."

"Oh! So you're already married?"

"No—not married. My family in Russia—*mein* old mother and Feivel, *mein* doctor brother, and Berel the baby, he was already learning for a bookkeeper before the war."

The coarse peasant features were transformed with tenderness as he started to tell me the story of his loved ones in Russia.

"Seven years ago I came to America. I thought only to make quick money to send the ship-tickets for them all, but I fell into the hands of a cockroach boss.

"You know a cockroach boss is a *landsmann* that comes to meet the greenhorns by the ship. He made out he wanted to help me, but he only wanted to sweat me into my grave. Then came the war and I began to earn big wages; but they were driven away from their village and my money didn't get to them at all. And for more than a year I didn't know if my people were yet alive in the world."

He took a much-fingered, greasy envelop from his pocket. "That's the first letter I got from them in months. The bookkeeper boarder read it for me already till he's sick from it. Only read it for me over again," he begged as he handed it to me upside down.

The letter was from Smirsk, Poland, where the two brothers and their old mother had fled for refuge. It was the cry of despair—food—clothes—shoes—the cry of hunger and nakedness. His eyes filled and unheeding tears fell on his rough, trembling hands as I read.

"That I should have bread three times a day and them starving!" he gulped. "By each bite it chokes me. And when I put myself on my warm coat, it shivers in me when I think how they're without a shirt on their backs. I already sent them a big package of things, but until I hear from them I'm like without air in my lungs."

I wondered how, in their great need and in his great anxiety to supply it, he could think of English lessons or spare the little money to pay for his tuition.

He divined my thoughts. "Already seven years I'm here and I didn't take for myself the time to go night-school," he explained. "Now they'll come soon and I don't want them to shame themselves from their *Ameri-kaner* brother what can't sign his own name, and they in Russia write me such smart letters in English."

"Didn't you go to school like your brothers?"

"Me—school?" He shrugged his toil-stooped shoulders. "I was the only bread-giver after my father he died. And with my nose in the earth on a farm how could I take myself the time to learn?"

His queer, bulging eyes with their yearning, passionate look seemed to cling to something beyond—out of reach. "But my brothers—ach! my brothers! They're so high educated! I worked the nails from off my fingers, but only they should learn—they should become people in the world."

And he deluged me with questions as to the rules of immigrant admission and how long it would take for him to learn to sign his name so that he would be a competent leader when his family would arrive.

I ain't so dumb like I look on my face." He nudged me confidentially. "I already found out from myself which picture means where the train goes. If it's for Brooklyn Bridge, then the hooks go this way"—he clumsily drew in the air with his thick fingers—"And if it's for the South Ferry then the words twist the other way around."

I marveled at his frank revelation of himself.

"What is your work?" I asked, more and more drawn by some hidden power of this simple peasant.

"I'm a presser by pants."

Now I understood the cause of the stooped, rounded shoulders. It must have come from pounding away with a heavy iron at an ironing board, day after day, year after year. But for all the ravages of poverty, of mean, soul-crushing drudgery that marked this man, something big and indomitable in him fascinated me. His was the strength knitted and knotted from the hardiest roots of the earth. Filled with awe, I looked up at him. Here was a man submerged in the darkness of illiteracy—of pinch and scraping and want—yet untouched—unspoiled, with the same simplicity of spirit that was his as a wide-eyed, dreamy youth in the green fields of Russia.

We had our first lesson, and, tho I needed every cent I could earn, I felt like a thief taking his precious pennies. But he would pay. "It's worth to me more than a quarter only to learn how to hold up the pencil," he exulted as he gripped the pencil upright in his thick fist. All the yearning, the intense desire for education were in the big, bulging eyes that he raised toward me. "No wonder I could never make those little black hooks for words; I was always grabbing my pencil like a fork for sticking up meat."

With what sublime absorption he studied me as I showed him how to shape the letters for his name! Eyes wide—mouth open—his huge, stoop-shouldered body leaning forward—quivering with hunger to grasp the secret turnings of "the little black hooks" that signified his name.

"M-o-i-s-h-e-h," he repeated after me as I guided his pencil.

"Now do it alone," I urged.

Moisheh rolled up his sleeve like one ready for a fray. The sweat dripped from his face as he struggled for the muscular control of his clumsy fingers.

Night after night he wrestled heroically with the "little black hooks." At last his efforts were rewarded. He learned how to shape the letters without any help.

"God from the world!" he cried with childishly pathetic joy as he wrote his name for the first time. "This is me—Moisheh!" He lifted the paper and held it off and then held it close, drunk with the wonder of the "little black hooks." They seemed so mysterious to him, and his eyes loomed large—transfigured with the miracle of seeing himself for the first time in script.

It was the week after that he asked me to write his letter, and this time it was from my eyes that the unheeding tears dropped as I wrote the words he dictated.

To my dear Loving Mother, and to my worthy Honorable Brother Feivel, the Doctor, and to my youngest brother, the joy from my life, the light from mine eyes, Berel, the Bookkeeper!

Long years and good luck to you all. Thanks the highest One in Heaven that you are alive. Don't worry for nothing. So long I have yet my two strong hands to work you will yet live to have from everything plenty. For all those starving days in Russia, you will live to have joy in America.

You, Feivel, will yet have a grand doctor's office, with an electric dentist sign over your door, and a gold tooth to pull in the richest customers. And you, Berel, my honorable bookkeeper, will yet live to wear a white starched collar like all the higher-ups in America. And you, my loving mother, will yet shine up the block with the joy from your children.

I am sending you another box of things, and so soon as I get from you the word, I'll send for you the ship-tickets, even if it costs the money from all the banks in America.

Luck and blessings on your dear heads. I am going around praying and counting the minutes till you are all with me together in America.

Our lessons had gone on steadily for some months and already he was able to write the letters of the alphabet. One morning before I was out of bed he knocked at my door.

"Quick only! A blue letter printed from Russia!" he shouted in an excited voice.

Through the crack of the door he shoved in the cablegram. "Send ship-tickets or we die—pogrom," I read aloud.

"Weh—weh!" A cry of a dumb wounded animal broke from the panic-stricken Moisheh.

The cup of coffee that Hanneh Breineh lifted to her lips dropped with a crash to the floor. "Where pogrom?" she demanded, rushing in.

I reread the cablegram.

"Money for ship-tickets!" stammered Moisheh. He drew forth a sweaty money-bag that lay hid beneath his torn gray shirt and with trembling hands began counting the greasy bills. "Only four hundred and thirty-three dollars! Woe is me!" He cracked the knuckles of his fingers in a paroxysm of grief. "It's six hundred I got to have!"

"*Gottuniu!* Listen to him only!" Hanneh Breineh shook Moisheh roughly. "You'd think he was living by wild Indians—not by people with hearts. . . .

"Boarders!" she called. "Moisheh's old mother and his two brothers are in Smirsk where there's a pogrom."

The word "pogrom" struck like a bombshell. From the sink, the stove, they gathered, in various stages of undress, around Moisheh, electrified into one bond of suffering brotherhood.

Hanneh Breineh, hand convulsively clutching her breast, began an impassioned appeal. "Which from us here needs me to tell what's a pogrom? It drips yet the blood from my heart when I only begin to remember. Only nine years old I was—the *pogromschiks* fell on our village. . . . Frightened! . . . You all know what's to be frightened from death—frightened from being burned alive or torn to pieces by wild wolves—but what's that compared to the cold shiverings that shook us by the hands and feet when we heard the drunken Cossacks coming nearer and nearer our hut. The last second my mother, like a crazy, pushed me and my little sister into the chimney. We heard the house tremble with shots— cries from my mother—father—then stillness. In the middle of the black night my little sister and I crawled ourselves out to see—" Hanneh Breineh covered her eyes as tho to shut out the hideous vision.

A pause.... Everybody heard everybody's heart beating. Before our eyes burned the terrible memory which Hanneh Breineh had tried to shut out and tried in vain....

Again Hanneh Breineh's voice arose. "I got no more breath for words—only this—the last bite from our mouths, the last shirt from our backs we got to take away to help out Moisheh. It's not only Moisheh's old mother that's out there—it's our own old mother—our own flesh-and-blood brothers.... Even I—beggar that I am—even I will give my only feather bed to the pawn."

A hush, and then a tumult of suppressed emotions. The room seethed with wild longings of the people to give—to help—to ease their aching hearts sharing Moisheh's sorrow.

Shoolem, a gray, tottering ragpicker, brought forth a grimy cigar box full of change. "Here is all the pennies and nickels and dimes I was saving and saving myself for fifteen years. I was holding by life on one hope—the hope that some day I would yet die before the holy walls from Jerusalem." With the gesture of a Rothschild he waved it in the air as he handed it over. "But here you got it, Moisheh. May it help to bring your brothers in good luck to America!"

Sosheh, the finisher, turned aside as she dug into her stocking and drew forth a crisp five-dollar bill. "That all I got till my next pay. Only it should help them," she gulped. "I wish I had somebody left alive that I could send a ship-ticket to."

Zaretzky, the matchmaker, snuffed noisily a pinch of tobacco and pulled from his overcoat pocket a book of War Savings stamps. "I got fourteen dollars of American

Liberty. Only let them come in good luck and I'll fix them out yet with the two grandest girls in New York."

The ship bearing Moisheh's family was to dock the next morning at eleven o'clock. The night before Hanneh Breineh and all of us were busy decorating the house in honor of the arrivals. The sound of hammering and sweeping and raised, excited voices filled the air.

Sosheh, the finisher, standing on top of a soapbox, was garnishing the chandelier with red-paper flowers.

Hanneh Breineh tacked bright, checked oilcloth on top of the wash-tubs.

Zaretzky was nailing together the broken leg of the table.

"I should live so," laughed Sosheh, her sallow face flushed with holiday joy. "This kitchen almost shines like a parlor, but for only this—"pointing to the sagging lounge where the stained mattress protruded.

"Shah! I'll fix this up in a minute so it'll look like new from the store." And Hanneh Breineh took out the red-flowered, Sabbath tablecloth from the bureau and tucked it around the lounge.

Meantime Moisheh, his eyes popping with excitement, raised clouds of dust as he swept dirt that had been gathering since Passover from the corners of the room.

Unable to wait any longer for the big moment, he had been secretly planning for weeks, zip! under the bed went the mountain of dirt, to be followed by the broom, which he kicked out of sight.

"Enough with the cleaning!" he commanded. "Come only around," and he pulled out from the corner his Russian steamer-basket.

"Oi—oi—oi—oi, and ai—ai!" the boarders shouted,

hilariously. "Will you treat us to a holiday cake maybe?"

"Wait only!" He gesticulated grandly as he loosened the lock.

One by one he held up and displayed the treasured trousseau which little by little he had gathered together for his loved ones.

A set of red-woolen underwear for each of the brothers, and for his mother a thick, gray shirt. Heavy cotton socks, a blue-checked apron, and a red-velvet waist appeared next. And then—Moisheh was reduced to gutteral grunts of primitive joy as he unfolded a rainbow tie for Feivel, the doctor, and pink suspenders for his "baby" brother.

Moisheh did not remove his clothes—no sleep for him that night. It was still dark when the sound of his heavy shoes, clumping around the kitchen as he cooked his breakfast, woke the rest of us.

"You got to come with me—I can't hold myself together with so much joy," he implored. There was no evading his entreaties, so I promised to get away as soon as I could and meet him at the dock.

I arrived at Ellis Island to find Moisheh stamping up and down like a wild horse. "What are they holding them so long?" he cried, mad with anxiety to reach those for whom he had so long waited and hungered.

I had to shake him roughly before I could make him aware of my presence, and immediately he was again lost in his eager search of the mob that crowded the gates.

The faces of the immigrants, from the tiniest babe at its mother's breast to the most decrepit old gray-haired man, were all stamped with the same transfigured look—a look of those who gazed for the first time upon the radiance of the dawn. The bosoms of the women heaved with excitement. The men seemed to be expanding, growing with the surge of realized hopes, of dreams come true. They inhaled deeply, eager to fill their stifled bodies and souls with the first life-giving breath of free air. Their eyes were luminous with hope, bewildered joy and vague forebodings. A voice was heard above the shouted orders and shuffling feet—above the clamor of the pressing crowds—*"Gott sei dank!"* The paean of thanksgiving was echoed and reechoed—a paean of nations released—America.

I had to hold tight to the bars not to be trampled underfoot by the crowd that surged through the gates. Suddenly a wild animal cry tore from Moisheh's throat. *"Mammeniu! Mammeniu!"* And a pair of gorilla-like arms infolded a gaunt, wasted little figure wrapped in a shawl.

"Moisheh! my heart!" she sobbed, devouring him with hunger-ravaged eyes.

"Ach!" she trembled—drawing back to survey her first-born. "From the bare feet and rags of Smirsk to leather shoes and a suit like a Rothschild!" she cried in Yiddish. *"Ach!*—I lived to see America!"

A dumb thing laughing and crying he stood there, a primitive figure, pathetic, yet sublime in the purity of his passionate love, his first love—his love for his mother.

The toil-worn little hand pulled at his neck as she whispered in Moisheh's ear, and as in a dream he turned with outstretched arms to greet his brothers.

"Feivel—*mein* doctor!" he cried.

"Yes, yes, we're here," said the high-browed young doctor in a tone that I thought was a little impatient. "Now let's divide up these bundles and get started." Moisheh's willing arms reached out for the heaviest sack.

"And here is my *teacherin!*" Moisheh's grin was that of a small boy displaying his most prized possession.

Berel, the baby, with the first down of young man-
hood still soft on his cheeks, shyly enveloped my hand
in his long sensitive fingers. "How nice for you to come—
a *teacherin*—an *Amerikanerin!*"

"Well—are we going?" came imperiously from
the doctor.

"Yeh—yeh!" answered Moisheh. "I'm so out of my
head from joy, my feet don't work." And, gathering the
few remaining lighter packages together, we threaded
our way through the crowded streets—the two newly
arrived brothers walking silently together.

"Has Moisheh changed much?" I asked the doctor as
I watched the big man help his mother tenderly across
the car tracks.

"The same Moisheh," he said, with an amused,
slightly superior air.

I looked at Berel to see if he was of the same cloth as
the doctor, but he was lost in dreamy contemplation of
the towering skyscrapers.

"Like granite mountains—the tower of Babel," Berel
mused aloud.

"How do they ever walk up to the top?" asked the
bewildered old mother.

"Walk!" cried Moisheh, overjoyed at the chance to
hand out information. "There are elevators in America.
You push a button and up you fly like on wings."

Elated with this opportunity to show off his superior
knowledge, he went on: "I learned myself to sign my
name in America. Stop only and I'll read for you the sign
from the lamp post," and he spelled aloud, "W-a-l-l—
Wall."

"And what street is this?" asked the doctor, as we
came to another corner.

Moisheh colored with confusion, and the eyes he

raised to his brother were like the eyes of a trapped deer pleading to be spared. "L-i-b—" He stopped. "Oh, *weh!*" he groaned, "the word is too long for me."

"Liberty," scorned the doctor. "You are an *Amerikaner* already and you don't know Liberty?"

His own humiliation forgot in pride of his brother's knowledge, Moisheh nodded his head humbly.

"Yeh—yeh! You are greener and yet you know Liberty. And I, an *Amerikaner,* is stuck by the word." He turned to me with a pride that brought tears to his eyes. "Didn't I tell you my brothers were high educated? Never mind—they won't shame me in America."

A look of adoration drank in the wonder of his beloved family. Overcome with a sense of his own unworthiness, he exclaimed, "Look only on me—a nothing and a nobody." He breathed in my ear, "And such brothers!" With a new, deeper tenderness, he pressed his mother's slight form more closely to him.

"More Bolsheviki!" scoffed a passerby.

"Trotzky's ambassadors," sneered another.

And the ridicule was taken up by a number of jeering voices.

"Poor devils!" came from a richly dressed Hebrew, resplendent in his fur collar and a diamond stud. There was in his eyes a wistful, reminiscent look. Perhaps the sight of these immigrants brought back to him the day he himself had landed, barefoot and in rags, with nothing but his dreams of America.

The street was thronged with hurrying lunch-seekers as we reached lower Broadway. I glanced at Moisheh's brothers, and I could not help noticing how different was the calm and carefree expression of their faces from the furtive, frantic acquisitive look of the men in the financial district.

But the moment we reached our block the people from the stoops and windows waved their welcome. Hanneh Breineh and all the boarders, dressed up in their best, ran to meet us.

"Home!" cried the glowing Moisheh. "*Mazeltuff.* Good luck!" answered Hanneh Breineh.

Instantly we were surrounded by the excited neighbors whose voices of welcome rose above the familiar cries of the hucksters and pedlers that lined the street.

"Give a help!" commanded Hanneh Breineh as she seized the bundles from Moisheh's numbed arms and divided them among the boarders. Then she led the procession triumphantly into her kitchen.

The table, with a profusion of festive dishes, sang aloud its welcome.

"Rockefeller's only daughter couldn't wish herself grander eatings by her own wedding," bragged the hostess as she waved the travelers to the feast. A brass pot filled with *gefullte fisch* was under the festooned chandelier. A tin platter heaped high with chopped liver and onions sent forth its inviting aroma. *Tzimmes—blintzes—* a golden-roasted goose swimming in its own fat ravished the senses. Eyes and mouths watered at sight of such luscious plenty.

"White bread!—*Ach!*—white bread!" gasped the hunger-ravaged old mother. Reaching across the table, she seized the loaf in her trembling hands. "All those starving years—all those years!" she moaned, kissing its flaky whiteness as tho it were a living thing.

"Sit yourself down—*mutterel!*" Hanneh Breineh soothed the old woman and helped her into the chair of honor. "White bread—even white bread is nothing in America. Even the charities—a black year on them— even the charities give white bread to the beggars."

Moisheh, beaming with joy of his loved ones' nearness, was so busy passing and repassing the various
dishes to his folks that he forgot his own meal.

"*Nu*—ain't it time for you also to sit yourself down
like a person?" urged Hanneh Breineh.

"*Takeh—takeh!*" added his mother. "Take something
to your mouth."

Thereupon Moisheh rolled up his sleeves and with
the zest of a hungry cave-man attacked the leg of a
goose. He no sooner finished than he bent ravenously
over the meat-platter, his forehead working with
rhythm to his jaws.

"Excuse me," stammered Moisheh, wiping his lips
with the end of his shirt-sleeve and sticking the meat
on a fork.

"What's the difference how you eat so long you got
what to eat?" broke in Zaretzky, grabbing the breast of
the goose and holding it up to his thick lips.

His sensibilities recoiling at this cannibalistic devouring of food, Berel rose and walked to the air-shaft
window. His arms shot out as tho to break down the
darkening wall which blotted out the daylight from the
little room. "Plenty of food for the body, but no light for
the soul," he murmured, not intending to be heard.

Feivel, the doctor, lit a cigaret and walked up and
down the room restlessly. He stopped and faced his
younger brother with a cynical smile. "I guess America
is like the rest of the world—you get what you take—
sunlight as well as other things—"

"How take sunlight? What do you mean?"

"I mean America is like a dish of cheese *blintzes* at a
poor-house. The beggars who are the head of the table
and get their hands in first, they live and laugh—"

Hanneh Breineh wiped her lips with the corner of

her apron and faced him indignantly. "You ain't yet finished with your first meal in America and already you're blowing from yourself like it's coming to you yet better."

"But why come to America?" defended Berel, the poet, "unless it gives you what's lacking in other lands? Even in the darkest days in Russia the peasants had light and air."

"Hey, Mr. Greenhorn Doctor—and you, young feller," broke in Zaretzky, the block politician, "if you don't like it here then the President from America will give you a free ride back on the same ship on which you came from."

Silenced by Zaretzky's biting retort, the doctor lit a cigaret and sent leisurely clouds of smoke ceilingward.

Moisheh, who had been too absorbed in his food to follow the talk, suddenly looked up from his plate. Tho unable to grasp the trend of the conversation, he intuitively sensed the hostile feeling in the room.

"Why so much high language," he asked, "when there's yet the nuts and raisins and the almonds to eat?"

A few months later Hanneh Breineh came into my room while peeling potatoes in her apron. "Greenhorns ain't what greenhorns use to be," she said, as she sat down on the edge of my cot. "Once when greenhorns came, a bone from a herring, a slice from an onion, was to them milk and honey; and now pour golden chicken-fat into their necks, and they turn up their nose like it's coming to them yet better."

"What is it now?" I laughed.

Hanneh Breineh rose. "Listen only to what is going on," she whispered, as she noiselessly pushed open the door and winked to me to come over and hear.

"I'm yet in debt over my neck. In God's name, how could you spend out so much money for only a little pleasure," remonstrated Moisheh.

"Do you think I'm a *schnorrer* like you? I'm a man, and I have to live," retorted the doctor.

"But two dollars for one evening in the opera only, when for ten cents you could have seen the grandest show in the movies!"

The doctor's contemptuous glance softened into a look of condescending pity. "After all, my presser of pants, what a waste the opera would be on you. Your America's the movies."

"Two dollars!" cried the little old mother, wringing her hands despairingly. "Moisheh didn't yet pay out for the ship-tickets."

"Ship-tickets—bah!—I wish he had never brought us to this golden country—dirt, darkness, houses like stalls for cattle!" And in a fury of disgust, not unmitigated with shame at his loss of temper, he slammed the door behind him.

"*Oi weh!*" wailed the care-worn old mother. "Two dollars for an opera, and in such bad times!"

"*Ach! Mammeniu,*" Moisheh defended, "maybe Feivel ain't like us. Remember he's high-educated. He needs the opera like I need the bite of bread. Maybe even more yet. I can live through without even the bite of bread, but Feivel must have what wills itself in him."

Hanneh Breineh closed the door and turned to me accusingly. "What's the use from all your education, if that's what kind of people it makes?"

"Yes," I agreed with Hanneh Breineh, "Education without heart is a curse."

Hanneh Breineh bristled. "I wish I should only be cursed with an education. It's only by the American education is nothing. It used to be an honor in Russia to shine a doctor's shoes for him."

"So you're for education, after all?" I ventured, trying the impossible—to pin Hanneh Breineh down.

"Blood-suckers!" Hanneh Breineh hissed. "Moisheh dries out the marrow from his head worrying for the dollar, and these high-educated brothers sit themselves on top of his neck like leeches. Greenhorns—opera—the world is coming to an end!"

Work with the Immigration Department took me to Washington for almost a year. As soon as I returned to New York I went to the only home I knew—Hanneh Breineh's lodging-house.

My old friend, Moisheh, greeted me at the door. *"Teacherin!"* he cried, with a shout of welcome, and then called to his mother. "Come quick. See only who is here!"

Sleeves rolled up and hands full of dough, the little soul hurried in. "The sky is falling to the earth!" she cried. "You here? And are you going to stay?"

"Sure will she stay," Moisheh, helping me remove my things.

"And where are Hanneh Breineh and the boarders?" I questioned.

"Out on a picnic by Coney Island."

"And why didn't you and your mother go?"

"I got to cook Feivel's dinner," she gesticulated with doughy palms.

"And I got my Coney Island here," said Moisheh.

To my great delight I saw he had been reading the life of Lincoln—the book I had left him the day I went away.

"My head is on fire thinking and dreaming from Lincoln. It shines before my face so real, I feel myself almost talking to him."

Moisheh's eyes were alive with light, and as I looked at him I felt for the first time a strange psychic resemblance between Moisheh and Lincoln. Could it be that the love for his hero had so transformed him as to him ost resemble him?

"Lincoln started life as a nothing and a nobody," Moisheh went on, dreamily, "and he made himself for the President from America—maybe there's yet a chance for me to make something from myself!"

"Sure there is. Show only what's in you and all America reaches out to help you."

"I used to think that I'd die a presser by pants. But since I read from Lincoln, something happened in me. I feel I got something for America—only I don't know how to give it out. I'm yet too much of a dummox—"

"What's in us must come out. I feel America needs you and me as much as she needs her Rockefellers and Morgans. Rockefellers and Morgans only pile up mountains of money; we bring to America the dreams and desires of ages—the youth that never had a chance to be young—the choked lives that never had a chance to live."

A shadow filmed Moisheh's brooding eyes. "I can't begin yet to think from myself for a few years. First comes my brothers. If only Feivel would work for himself up for a big doctor and Berel for a big writer then I'll feel myself free to do something...."

"Shah! I got great news for you," Moisheh announced. "Feivel has already his doctor's office."

"Where did he get all the money?"

"On the installment plan I got him the chair and the office things. Now he's beginning to earn already enough to pay almost half his rent."

"Soon he'll be for dinner." The old lady jumped up. "I got to get his eating ready before he comes." And she hastened back to the kitchen stove.

"And Berel—what does he do?" I inquired.

"Berel ain't working yet. He's still writing from his head," explained Moisheh. "Wait only and I'll call him. He's locked himself up in his bedroom; nobody should bother him."

"Berel!" he called, tapping respectfully at the door.

"*Yuk!*" came in a voice of nervous irritation. "What is it?"

"The *teacherin* is here," replied Moisheh. "Only a minute."

"It's me," I added. "I'd like to see you."

Berel came out, hair disheveled, with a dreamy, absent look, holding pencil and paper in his hand. "I was just finishing a poem," he said in greeting to me.

"I have been looking for your name in the magazines. Have you published anything yet?"

"I—publish in the American magazines?" he flung, hurt beyond words. "I wouldn't mix my art with their empty drivel."

"But, surely, there are some better magazines," I protested.

"Pshah! Their best magazines—the pink-and-white jingles that they call poetry are not worth the paper they're printed on. America don't want poets. She wants plumbers."

"But what will you do with the poetry you write?"

"I'll publish it myself. Art should be free, like sunlight and beauty. The only compensation for the artist is the chance to feed hungry hearts. If only Moisheh could give me the hundred dollars I'd have my volume printed at once."

"But how can I raise all the money when I'm not yet paid out with Feivel's doctor's office?" remonstrated

Moisheh. "Don't you think if—maybe you'd get a little job?"

An expression of abstraction came over Berel's face, and he snapped, impatiently: "Yes—yes—I told you that I would look for a job. But I must write this while I have the inspiration."

"Can't you write your inspiration out in the evening?" faltered Moisheh. "If you could only bring in a few dollars a week to help pay ourselves out to the installment man."

Berel looked at his brother with compassionate tolerance. "What are to you the things of the soul? All you care for is money—money—money! You'd want me to sell my soul, my poetry, my creative fire—to hand you a few dirty dollars."

The postman's whistle and the cry, "Berel Pinski!"

Moisheh hurried downstairs and brought back a large return envelope.

"Another one of those letters back," deplored the mother, untactfully. "You're only making the post-office rich with the stamps from Moisheh's blood money."

"Dammit!" Defeat enraged the young poet to the point of brutality. "Stop nagging me and mixing in with things you don't understand!" He struck the rude table with his clenched fist. "It's impossible to live with you thickheads—numskulls—money-grubbing worms."

He threw on his hat and coat and paused for a moment glowering in the doorway. "Moisheh," he demanded, "give me a quarter for carfare. I have to go uptown to the library." Silently the big brother handed him the money, and Berel flung himself out of the room.

The door had no sooner closed on the poet than the doctor sauntered into the room. After a hasty "Hello," he turned to Moisheh. "I have a wonderful chance—but I can't take advantage of it."

"What!" cried Moisheh, his face brightening.

"My landlord invited me to his house to-night, to meet his only daughter."

"Why not go?" demanded Moisheh.

"Sure you got to go," urged the mother, as she placed the food before him. "The landlord only got to see how smart you are and he'll pull you in the richest customers from uptown."

Feivel looked at his clothes with resigned contempt. "H—m," he smiled bitterly. "Go in this shabby suit? I have too much respect for myself."

There was troubled silence. Both brother and mother were miserable that their dear one should be so deprived.

Moisheh moved over to the window, a worried look on his face. Presently he turned to his brother. "I'd give you the blood from under my nails for you but I'm yet so behind with the instalment man."

The doctor stamped his foot impatiently. "I simply have to have a suit! It's a question of life and death.... Think of the chance! The landlord took a liking to me— rich as Rockefeller—and an only daughter. If he gives me a start in an uptown office I could *coin* money. All I need is a chance—the right location. Ten—twenty— fifty dollars an hour. There's no limit to a dentist's fee. If he sets me up on Riverside Drive I could charge a hundred dollars for work I get five for in Rutgers Street!"

"Can I tear myself in pieces? Squeeze the money from my flesh?"

"But do you realize that, once I get uptown, I could earn more in an hour that you could in a month? I'll pay you back every penny a hundred times over."

"*Nu*—tell me only—what can I do? Anything you'll say—"

"Why—you have your gold watch."

Moisheh's hand leaped to the watch in his vest poc-

ket. "My gold watch! My prize from the night-school?"
he pleaded. "It ain't just a watch—it's given me by the
principal for never being absent for a whole year."

"Oh, rot!—you, with your sentimentality! Try to
understand something once." The doctor waved his
objections aside. "Once I get my start in an uptown office I can buy you a dozen watches. I'm telling you my
whole future depends on the front I put up at the landlord's house, and still you hesitate!"

Moisheh looked at his watch, fingering it tenderly.
"*Oi weh!*" he groaned "It's like a piece from my heart.
My prize from the night-school," he mumbled, brokenly;
"but take it if you got to have it."

"You'll get it back," confidently promised the doctor,
"get it back a hundred times over." And as he slipped
the watch into his pocket, Moisheh's eyes followed it
doggedly. "So long, *mammeniu;* no dinner for me to-day."
Feivel bestowed a hasty good-by caress upon his
old mother.

The doctor was now living in an uptown boarding
house, having moved some weeks before, giving the
excuse that for his business it was necessary to cultivate
an uptown acquaintance. But he still kept up his office
in Rutgers Street.

One morning after he had finished treating my
teeth, he took up a cigaret, nervously lit it, attempted
to smoke, and then threw it way. I had never seen the
suave, complacent man so unnerved and fidgety.
Abruptly he stopped in front of me and smiled almost
affectionately.

"You are the very person I want to speak to this
morning—you are the only person I want to speak to,"
he repeated.

I was a little startled, for this manner was most un-
like him. Seldom did he even notice me, just as he did
not notice most of Moisheh's friends. But his exuberant
joyousness called out my instinctive response, and before
I knew it I was saying, "If there's anything I can do for
you I'll be only too happy."

He took a bill from his pocket, placed it in my hand,
and said, with repressed excitement: "I want you to take
my mother and Moisheh to see 'Welcome Stranger.' It's
a great show. It's going to be a big night with me, and I
want them to be happy, too."

I must have looked puzzled, for he narrowed his
eyes and studied me, twice starting to speak, and both
times stopping himself.

"You must have thought me a selfish brute all this
time," he began. "But I've only been biding my time. I
must make the most of myself, and now is my only
chance—to rise in the world."

He stopped again, paced the floor several times,
placed a chair before me, and said: "Please sit down. I
want to talk to you."

There was a wistful pleading in his voice that none
could resist, and for the first time I was aware of the
compelling humanness of this arrogant intellectual.

"I'll tell you everything just as it is," he started. And
then he stopped again. *"Ach!"* he groaned. "There's
something I would like to talk over with you—but I just
can't. You wouldn't understand. . . . A great thing is happening in my life to-night—but I can't confide it to anyone—none can understand. But—I ask of you just this:
Will you give Moisheh and my mother a good time? Let
the poor devils enjoy themselves for once!"

As I walked out of the office, the bill still crumpled
in my hand, I reproached myself for my former harsh

condemnation of the doctor. Perhaps all those months, when I had thought him so brutally selfish, he had been building for the future.

But what was this mysterious good fortune that he could not confide to any one—and that none could understand?

"Doctor Feivel gave me money to take you to the theater," I announced as I entered the house.

"Theater!" chorused Moisheh and his mother, excitedly.

"Yes," I said. "Feivel seemed so happy to-day, and he wanted you to share his happiness."

"Feivel, the golden heart!" The old mother's eyes were misty with emotion.

"*Ach!* Didn't I tell you even if my brother is high-educated, he won't shame himself from us?" Moisheh faced me triumphantly. "I was so afraid since he moved himself into an uptown boarding house that maybe we are losing him, even tho he still kept up his office on Rutgers Street." Moisheh's eyes shone with delight.

"I'll tell you a little secret," said he, leaning forward confidentially. "I'm planning to give a surprise to Feivel. In another month I'll pay myself out for the last of Feivel's office things. And for days and nights I'm going around thinking and dreaming about buying him an electric sign. Already I made the price with the instalment man for it." By this time his recital was ecstatic. "And think only—what *mein* doctor will say, when he'll come one morning from his uptown boarding house and find my grand surprise waiting for him over his office door!"

All the way to the theater Moisheh and his mother drank in the glamour and the glitter of the electric signs of Broadway.

"*Gottuniu!* If I only had the money for such a sign for Feivel," Moisheh sighed, pointing to the chewing-gum advertisement on the roof of a building near the Astor. "If I only had Rockefeller's money. I'd light up America with Feivel's doctor-sign!"

When we reached the theater, we found we had come almost an hour too early.

"Never mind—*mammeniu!*" Moisheh took his mother's arm tenderly. "We'll have time now to walk ourselves along and see the riches and lights from America."

"I should live so," he said, surveying his mother affectionately. "That red velvet waist and this new shawl over your head makes your face so shine, everybody stops to give a look on you."

"Yeh—yeh! You're always saying love words to every woman you see."

"But this time it's my mother, so I mean it from my heart."

Moisheh nudged me confidentially. "*Teacherin!* See only how a little holiday lifts up my *mammeniu!* Don't it dance from her eyes the joy like from a young girl?"

"Stop already making fun from your old mother."

"You old?" Moisheh put his strong arm around his mother's waist. "Why, people think we're a young couple on our honeymoon."

"Honeymoon—*ach!*" The faded face shone with inward visioning. "My only wish is to see for my eyes my sons marry themselves in good luck. What's my life—but only the little hope from my children? To dance with the bride on my son's wedding will make me the happiest mother from America."

"Feivel will soon give you that happiness," responded Moisheh. "You know how the richest American-born girls are trying to catch on to him. And no matter how grand the girl he'll marry himself to, you'll have the first place of honor by the wedding."

As we turned in at Forty-fifth Street a curious crowd blocked our path. A row of sleek limousines stood before the arched entrance of the Van Suydden Hotel.

"Look only—a wedding! Let's give a look on the bride!" exclaimed Moisheh's mother, eagerly. A wedding was, in her religion, the most significant ceremony in life. And for her sake we elbowed our way toward the front.

A procession of bridesmaids in shimmering chiffons, bedecked with flowers, were the first to tread the carpeted steps.

Then we saw the bride... And then—Good God!—was it possible?

Moisheh clutched his mother's hand convulsively. Could it really be their Feivel?

The two stood gaping blindly, paralyzed by the scene before them.

Suddenly—roused by the terrible betrayal—the mother uttered a distorted sob of grief. "Feivel—son *mein!* What have you done to me?"

Moisheh grasped the old woman more firmly as the bride tossed her head and turned possessive eyes on her husband—their son and brother.

The onlookers murmured appreciatively, thrilled by the pretty romance.

Enraged by the stupid joy of the crowd which mocked her misery, the old mother broke from Moisheh's hold with wiry strength and clawed wildly at the people around her.

"Feivel—black curses—!" she hissed—and then she crumpled, fainting, into Moisheh's arms.

Unaware of the disturbance outside, the happy

couple passed into the festive reception-hall.

With quick self-control, Moisheh motioned to a taxi-cab out of which had just emerged another wedding-guest. Then he gently lifted the fainting form of the little mother in beside him.

And all through the night the bitter tears of betrayed motherhood poured over the shrunken bosom where Feivel, as a suckling infant, had once helped himself to life.

Where Lovers Dream

For years I was saying to myself—Just so you will act when you meet him. Just so you will stand. So will you look on him. These words you will say to him.

I wanted to show him that what he had done to me could not down me; that his leaving me the way he left me, that his breaking my heart the way he broke it, didn't crush me; that his grand life and my pinched-in life, his having learning and my not having learning— that the difference didn't count so much like it seemed; that on the bottom I was the same like him.

But he came upon me so sudden, all my plannings for years smashed to the wall. The sight of him was like an earthquake shaking me to pieces.

I can't yet see nothing in front of me and can't get my head together to anything, so torn up I am from the shock.

It was at Yetta Solomon's wedding I met him again. She was after me for weeks I should only come.

"How can I come to such a swell hall?" I told her. "You know I ain't got nothing decent to wear."

"Like you are without no dressing-up, I want you to come. You are the kind what people look in your eyes and not on what you got on. Ain't you yourself the one what helped me with my love troubles? And now, when everything is turning out happy, you mean to tell me that you ain't going to be there?"

She gave me a grab over and kissed me in a way that I couldn't say "No" to her.

So I shined myself up in the best I had and went to the wedding.

I was in the middle from giving my congratulations to Yetta and her new husband, when—Gott! Gott im Himmel! The sky is falling to the earth! I see him—him, and his wife leaning on his arm, coming over.

I gave a fall back, like something sharp hit me. My head got dizzy, and my eyes got blind.

I wanted to run away from him, but, ach! everything in me rushed to him.

I was feeling like struck deaf, dumb, and blind all in one.

He must have said something to me, and I must have answered back something to him, but how? What? I only remember like in a dream my getting to the cloakroom. Such a tearing, grinding pain was dragging me down to the floor that I had to hold on to the wall not to fall.

All of a sudden I feel a pull on my arm. It was the janitor with the broom in his hand.

"Lady, are you sick? The wedding people is all gone, and I swept up already."

"But I couldn't wake up from myself.

"Lady, the lights is going out," he says, looking on me queer.

"I think I ain't well," I said. And I went out.

Ach, I see again the time when we was lovers! How beautiful the world was then!

"Maybe there never was such love like ours, and never will be," we was always telling one another.

When we was together there was like a light shining around us, the light from his heart on mine, and from my heart on his. People began to look happy just looking on us.

When we was walking we didn't feel we was touching

the earth but flying high up through the air. We looked on the rest of the people with pity, because it was seeming to us that we was the only two persons awake, and all the rest was hurrying and pushing and slaving and crowding one on the other without the splendidness of feeling for what it was all for, like we was feeling it.

David was learning for a doctor. Daytimes he went to college, and nights he was in a drugstore. I was working in a factory on shirtwaists. We was poor. But we didn't feel poor. The waists I was sewing flyed like white birds through my fingers, because his face was shining out of everything I touched.

David was always trying to learn me how to make myself over for an American. Sometimes he would spend out fifteen cents to buy me the *Ladies' Home Journal* to read about American life, and my whole head was put away on how to look neat and be up-to-date like the American girls. Till long hours in the night I used to stay up brushing and pressing my plain blue suit with the white collar what David liked, and washing my waists, and fixing up my hat like the pattern magazines show you.

On holidays he took me out for a dinner by a restaurant to learn how the Americans eat, with napkins, and use up so many plates—the butter by itself, and the bread by itself, and the meat by itself, and the potatoes by itself.

Always when the six o'clock whistle blowed, he was waiting for me on the corner from the shop to take me home.

"Ut, there waits Sara's doctor feller," the girls were nudging one to the other, as we went out from the shop. "Ain't she the lucky one!"

All the way as we walked along he was learning me

how to throw off my greenhorn talk, and say out the words in the American.

He used to stop me in the middle of the pavement and laugh from me, shaking me: "No t'ink or t'ank or t'ought, now. You're an American," he would say to me. And then he would fix my tongue and teeth together and make me say after him: "th-think, th-thank, th-thought; this, that, there." And if I said the words right, he kissed me in the hall when we got home. And if I said them wrong, he kissed me anyhow.

He moved next door to us, so we shouldn't lose the sweetness from one little minute that we could be together. There was only the thin wall between our kitchen and his room, and the first thing in the morning, we would knock in one to the other to begin the day together.

"See what I got for you, Hertzele," he said to me one day, holding up a grand printed card.

I gave a read. It was the ticket invitation for his graduation from college. I gave it a touch, with pride melting over in my heart.

"Only one week more, and you'll be a doctor for the world!"

"And then, heart of mine," he said, drawing me over to him and kissing me on the lips, "when I get my office fixed up, you will marry me?"

"Ach, such a happiness," I answered, "to be together all the time, and wait on you and cook for you, and do everything for you, like if I was your mother!"

"Uncle Rosenberg is coming special from Boston for my graduation."

"The one what helped out your chance for college?" I asked.

"Yes, and he's going to start me up the doctor's office, he says. Like his son he looks on me, because he only got daughters in his family."

"Ach, the good heart! He'll yet have joy and good luck from us! What is he saying about me?" I ask.

"I want him to see you first, darling. You can't help going to his heart, when he'll only give a look on you."

"Think only, Mammele—David is graduating for a doctor in a week!" I gave a hurry in to my mother that night. "And his Uncle Rosenberg is coming special from Boston and says he'll start him up in his doctor's office."

"Oi weh, the uncle is going to give a come, you say? Look how the house looks! And the children in rags and no shoes on their feet!"

The whole week before the uncle came, my mother and I was busy nights buying and fixing up, and painting the chairs, and nailing together solid the table, and hanging up calendar pictures to cover up the broken plaster on the wall, and fixing the springs from the sleeping lounge so it didn't sink in, and scrubbing up everything, and even washing the windows, like before Passover.

I stopped away from the shop, on the day David was graduating. Everything in the house was like for a holiday. The children shined up like rich people's children, with their faces washed clean and their hair brushed and new shoes on their feet. I made my father put away his black shirt and dress up in an American white shirt and starched collar. I fixed out my mother in a new white waist and a blue checked apron, and I blowed myself to dress up the baby in everything new, like a doll in a window. Her round, laughing face lighted up the house, so beautiful she was.

By the time we got finished the rush to fix ourselves out, the children's cheeks was red with excitement and our eyes was bulging bright, like ready to start for a picnic.

When David came in with his uncle, my father and mother and all the children gave a stand up.

But the "Boruch Chabo" and the hot words of welcome, what was rushing from us to say, froze up on our lips by the stiff look the uncle throwed on us.

David's uncle didn't look like David. He had a thick neck and a red face and the breathing of a man what eats plenty.—But his eyes looked smart like David's.

He wouldn't take no seat and didn't seem to want to let go from the door.

David laughed and talked fast, and moved around nervous, trying to cover up the ice. But he didn't get no answers from nobody. And he didn't look in my eyes, and I was feeling myself ashamed, like I did something wrong which I didn't understand.

My father started up to say something to the uncle— "Our David—" But I quick pulled him by the sleeve to stop. And nobody after that could say nothing, nobody except David.

I couldn't get up the heart to ask them to give a taste from the cake and the wine what we made ready special for them on the table.

The baby started crying for a cake, and I quick went over to take her up, because I wanted to hide myself with being busy with her. But only the crying and nothing else happening made my heart give a shiver, like bad luck was in the air.

And right away the uncle and him said goodbye and walked out.

When the door was shut the children gave a rush for the cakes, and then burst out in the street.

"Come, Schmuel," said my mother, "I got to say something with you." And she gave my father a pull in the other room and closed the door.

I felt they was trying not to look on me, and was

shrinking away from the shame that was throwed on me.

"Och, what's the matter with me! Nothing can come between David and me. His uncle ain't everything," I said, trying to pull up my head.

I sat myself down by the table to cool down my nervousness. "Brace yourself up," I said to myself, jumping up from the chair and beginning to walk around again. "Nothing has happened. Stop off nagging yourself."

Just then I hear loud voices through the wall. I go nearer. Ut, it's his uncle!

The plaster from the wall was broken on our side by the door. "Lay your ear in this crack, and you can hear plain the words," I say to myself.

"What's getting over you? You ain't that kind to do such a thing," I say. But still I do it.

Oi weh, I hear the uncle plainly! "What's all this mean, these neighbors? Who's the pretty girl what made such eyes on you?"

"Ain't she beautiful? Do you like her?" I hear David.

"What? What's the matter to you?"

"I'll marry myself to her," says David.

"Marry! Marry yourself into that beggar house! Are you crazy?"

"A man could get to anywhere with such a beautiful girl."

"Koosh! Pretty faces is cheap like dirt. What has she got to bring you in for your future? An empty pocketbook? A starving family to hang over your neck?"

"You don't know nothing about her. You don't know what you're saying. She comes from fine people in Russia. You can see her father is a learned man."

"Ach! You make me a disgust with your calf talk! Poverty winking from every corner of the house! Hunger hollering from all their starved faces! I got too much sense to waste my love on beggars. And all the time I was planning for you an American family, people which are somebodies in this world, which could help you work up a practice! For why did I waste my good dollars on you?"

"Gott! Ain't David answering?" my heart cries out. "Why don't he throw him out of the house?"

"Perhaps I can't hear him," I think, and with my fingernails I pick thinner the broken plaster.

I push myself back to get away and not to do it. But it did itself with my hands. "Don't let me hear nothing," I pray, and yet I strain more to hear.

"The uncle was still hollering. And David wasn't saying nothing for me.

"Gazlen! You want to sink your life in a family of beggars?"

"But I love her. We're so happy together. Don't that count for something? I can't live without her."

"Koosh! Love her! Do you want to plan your future with your heart or with your head? Take for your wife an ignorant shopgirl without a cent! Can two dead people start up a dance together?"

"So you mean not to help me with the office?"

"Yah-yah-yah! I'll run on all fours to do it! The impudence from such penniless nobodies wanting to pull in a young man with a future for a doctor! Nobody but such a yok like you would be such an easy mark."

"Well, I got to live my own life, and I love her."

"That's all I got to say.—Where's my hat? Throw yourself away on the pretty face, make yourself to shame and to laughter with a ragged Melamid for a father-in-law, and I wash my hands from you for the rest of your life."

A change came over David from that day. For the first time we was no more one person together. We couldn't no more laugh and talk like we used to. When I tried to look him in the eyes, he gave them a turn away from me.

I used to lie awake nights turning over in my head David's looks, David's words, and it made me frightened like something black rising over me and pushing me out from David's heart. I could feel he was blaming me for something I couldn't understand.

Once David asked me, "Don't you love me no more?"

I tried to tell him that there wasn't no change in my love, but I couldn't no more talk out to him what was in my mind, like I used to.

"I didn't want to worry you before with my worries," he said to me at last.

"Worry me, David! What am I here for?"

"My uncle is acting like a stingy grouch," he answered me, "and I can't stand no more his bossing me."

"Why didn't you speak yourself out to me what was on your mind, David?" I asked him.

"You don't know how my plans is smashed to pieces," he said, with a worried look on his face. "I don't see how I'll ever be able to open my doctor's office. And how can we get married with your people hanging on for your wages?"

"Ah, David, don't you no longer feel that love can find a way out?"

He looked on me, down and up, and up and down, till I drawed myself back, frightened.

But he grabbed me back to him. "I love you. I love you, heart of mine," he said, kissing me on the neck, on my hair and my eyes. "And nothing else matters, does it, does it?" and he kissed me again and again, as if he wanted to swallow me up.

Next day I got out from the shop and down the steps to meet him, like on every day.

I give a look around.

"Gott! Where is he? He wasn't never late before," gave a knock my heart.

I waited out till all the girls was gone, and the streets was getting empty, but David didn't come yet.

"Maybe an accident happened to him, and I standing round here like a dummy," and I gave a quick hurry home.

But nobody had heard nothing.

"He's coming! He *must* come!" I fighted back my fear. But by evening he hadn't come yet.

I sent in my brother next door to see if he could find him.

"He moved to-day," comes in my brother to tell me.

"My God! David left me? It ain't possible!"

I walk around the house, waiting and listening. "Don't let nobody see your nervousness. Don't let yourself out. Don't break down."

It got late and everybody was gone to bed.

I couldn't take my clothes off. Any minute he'll come up the steps or knock on the wall. Any minute a telegram will come.

It's twelve o'clock. It's one. Two!

Every time I hear footsteps in the empty street, I am by the window—"Maybe it's him."

It's beginning the day.

The sun is rising. Oi weh, how can the sun rise and he not here?

Mein Gott! He ain't coming!

I sit myself down on the floor by the window with my head on the sill.

Everybody is sleeping. I can't sleep. And I'm so tired.

Next day I go, like pushed on, to the shop, glad to be swallowed up by my work.

The noise of the knocking machines is like a sleeping-medicine to the cryings inside of me. All day I watched my hands push the waists up and down the machine. I wasn't with my hands. It was like my breathing stopped and I was sitting inside of myself, waiting for David.

The six o'clock whistle blowed. I go out from the shop. I can't help it—I look for him.

"Oi, Gott! Do something for me once! Send him only!"

I hold on to the iron fence of the shop, because I feel my heart bleeding away.

I can't go away. The girls all come out from the shops, and the streets get empty and still. But at the end of the block once in a while somebody crosses and goes out from sight.

I watch them. I begin counting, "One, two, three—"

Underneath my mind is saying, "Maybe it's him. Maybe the next one!"

My eyes shut themselves. I feel the end from everything.

"Ah, David! David! Gott! Mein Gott!"

I fall on the steps and clinch the stones with the twistings of my body. A terrible cry breaks out from me—"David! David!" My soul is tearing itself out from my body. It is gone.

Next day I got news—David opened a doctor's office uptown.

Nothing could hurt me no more. I didn't hope for nothing. Even if he wanted me back, I couldn't go to him no more. I was like something dying what wants to be left alone in darkness.

But still something inside of me wanted to see for itself how all is dead between us, and I write him:

"David Novak: You killed me. You killed my love. Why did you leave me yet living? Why must I yet drag on the deadness from me?"

I don't know why I wrote him. I just wanted to give a look on him. I wanted to fill up my eyes with him before I turned them away forever.

I was sitting by the table in the kitchen, wanting to sew, but my hands was lying dead on the table, when the door back of me burst open.

"O God! What have I done? Your face is like ashes! You look like you are dying!" David gave a rush in.

His hair wasn't combed, his face wasn't shaved, his clothes was all wrinkled. My letter he was holding crushed in his hand.

"I killed you! I left you! But I didn't rest a minute since I went away! Heart of mine, forgive me!"

He gave a take my hand, and fell down kneeling by me.

"Sarale, speak to me!"

"False dog! Coward!" cried my father, breaking in on us. "Get up! Get out! Don't dare touch my child again! May your name and memory be blotted out!"

David covered up his head with his arm and fell back to the wall like my father had hit him.

"You yet listen to him?" cried my father, grabbing me by the arm and shaking me. "Didn't I tell you he's a Meshumid, a denier of God?"

"Have pity! Speak to me! Give me only a word!" David begged me.

I wanted to speak to him, to stretch out my hands to him and call him over, but I couldn't move my body. No voice came from my lips no more than if I was locked in my grave.

I was dead, and the David I loved was dead.

I married Sam because he came along and wanted me, and I didn't care about nothing no more.

But for long after, even when the children began coming, my head was still far away in the dream of the time when love was. Before my eyes was always his face, drawing me on. In my ears was always his voice, but thin, like from far away.

I was like a person following after something in the dark.

For years when I went out into the street or got into a car, it gave a knock my heart—"Maybe I'll see him yet to-day."

When I heard he got himself engaged, I hunted up where she lived, and with Sammy in the carriage and the three other children hanging on to my skirts, I stayed around for hours to look up at the grand stone house where she lived, just to take a minute's look on her.

When I seen her go by, it stabbed awake in me the old days.

It ain't that I still love him, but nothing don't seem real to me no more. For the little while when we was lovers I breathed the air from the high places where love comes from, and I can't no more come down.

II

STRUGGLE

The Fat of the Land

In an air-shaft so narrow that you could touch the next wall with your bare hands, Hanneh Breineh leaned out and knocked on her neighbor's window.

"Can you loan me your wash-boiler for the clothes?" she called.

Mrs. Pelz threw up the sash.

"The boiler? What's the matter with yours again? Didn't you tell me you had it fixed already last week?"

"A black year on him, the robber, the way he fixed it! If you have no luck in this world, then it's better not to live. There I spent out fifteen cents to stop up one hole, and it runs out another. How I ate out my gall bargaining with him he should let it down to fifteen cents! He wanted yet a quarter, the swindler. Gottuniu! My bitter heart on him for every penny he took from me for nothing!"

"You got to watch all those swindlers, or they'll steal the whites out of your eyes," admonished Mrs. Pelz. "You should have tried out your boiler before you paid him. Wait a minute till I empty out my dirty clothes in a pillowcase; then I'll hand it to you."

Mrs. Pelz returned with the boiler and tried to hand it across to Hanneh Breineh, but the soapbox refrigerator on the window sill was in the way.

"You got to come in for the boiler yourself," said Mrs. Pelz.

"Wait only till I tie my Sammy on to the highchair he shouldn't fall on me again. He's so wild that ropes won't hold him."

Hanneh Breineh tied the child in the chair, stuck a

pacifier in his mouth, and went in to her neighbor. As she took the boiler Mrs. Pelz said:

"Do you know Mrs. Melker ordered fifty pounds of chicken for her daughter's wedding? And such grand chickens! Shining like gold! My heart melted in me just looking at the flowing fatness of those chickens."

Hanneh Breineh smacked her thin, dry lips, a hungry gleam in her sunken eyes.

"Fifty pounds!" she gasped. "It ain't possible. How do you know?"

"I heard her with my own ears. I saw them with my own eyes. And she said she will chop up the chicken livers with onions and eggs for an appetizer, and then she will buy twenty-five pounds of fish, and cook it sweet and sour with raisins, and she said she will bake all her shtrudels on pure chicken fat."

"Some people work themselves up in the world," sighed Hanneh Breineh. "For them is America flowing with milk and honey. In Savel, Mrs. Melker used to get shriveled up from hunger. She and her children used to live on potato-peelings and crusts of dry bread picked out from the barrels; and in America she lives to eat chicken, and apple shtrudels soaking in fat."

"The world is a wheel always turning," philosophized Mrs. Pelz. "Those who were high go down low, and those who've been low go up higher. Who will believe me here in America that in Poland I was a cook in a banker's house? I handled ducks and geese every day. I used to bake coffeecake with cream so thick you could cut it with a knife."

"And do you think I was a nobody in Poland?" broke in Hanneh Breineh, tears welling in her eyes as the memories of her past rushed over her. "But what's the use of talking? In America money is everything. Who cares who my father or grandfather was in Poland? Without money I'm a living dead one. My head dries out worrying how to get for the children the eating a penny cheaper."

Mrs. Pelz wagged her head, a gnawing envy contracting her features.

"Mrs. Melker had it good from the day she came," she said, begrudgingly. "Right away she sent all her children to the factory, and she began to cook meat for dinner every day. She and her children have eggs and buttered rolls for breakfast each morning like millionaires."

A sudden fall and a baby's scream, and the boiler dropped from Hanneh Breineh's hands as she rushed into her kitchen, Mrs. Pelz after her. They found the highchair turned on top of the baby.

"Gewalt! Save me! Run for a doctor!" cried Hanneh Breineh, as she dragged the child from under the highchair. "He's killed! He's killed! My only child! My precious lamb!" she shrieked as she ran back and forth with the screaming infant.

Mrs. Pelz snatched little Sammy from the mother's hands.

"Meshugeneh! What are you running around like a crazy, frightening the child? Let me see. Let me tend to him. He ain't killed yet." She hastened to the sink to wash the child's face, and discovered a swelling lump on his forehead. "Have you a quarter in your house?" she asked.

"Yes, I got one," replied Hanneh Breineh, climbing on a chair. "I got to keep it on a high shelf where the children can't get it."

Mrs. Pelz seized the quarter Hanneh Breineh handed down to her.

"Now pull your left eyelid three times while I'm

pressing the quarter, and you'll see the swelling go down."

Hanneh Breineh took the child again in her arms, shaking and cooing over it and caressing it.

"Ah-ah-ah, Sammy! Ah-ah-ah-ah, little lamb! Ah-ah-ah, little bird! Ah-ah-ah-ah, precious heart! Oh, you saved my life; I thought he was killed," gasped Hanneh Breineh, turning to Mrs. Pelz. "Oi-i!" she sighed, "a mother's heart! Always in fear over her children. The minute anything happens to them all life goes out of me. I lose my head and I don't know where I am anymore."

"No wonder the child fell," admonished Mrs. Pelz. "You should have a red ribbon or red beads on his neck to keep away the evil eye. Wait. I got something in my machine-drawer."

Mrs. Pelz returned, bringing the boiler and a red string, which she tied about the child's neck while the mother proceeded to fill the boiler.

A little later Hanneh Breineh again came into Mrs. Pelz's kitchen, holding Sammy in one arm and in the other an apronful of potatoes. Putting the child down on the floor, she seated herself on the unmade kitchen-bed and began to peel the potatoes in her apron.

"Woe to me!" sobbed Hanneh Breineh. "To my bitter luck there ain't no end. With all my other troubles, the stove got broke. I lighted the fire to boil the clothes, and it's to get choked with smoke. I paid rent only a week ago, and the agent don't want to fix it. A thunder should strike him! He only comes for the rent, and if anything has to be fixed, then he don't want to hear nothing.

"Why comes it to me so hard?" went on Hanneh Breineh, the tears streaming down her cheeks. "I can't stand it no more. I came in to you for a minute to run away from my troubles. It's only when I sit myself down to peel potatoes or nurse the baby that I take time to draw a breath, and beg only for death."

Mrs. Pelz, accustomed to Hanneh Breineh's bitter outbursts, continued her scrubbing.

"Ut!" exclaimed Hanneh Breineh, irritated at her neighbor's silence, "what are you tearing up the world with your cleaning? What's the use to clean up when everything only gets dirty again?"

"I got to shine up my house for the holidays."

"You've got it so good nothing lays on your mind but to clean your house. Look on this little bloodsucker," said Hanneh Breineh, pointing to the wizened child, made prematurely solemn from starvation and neglect. "Could anybody keep that brat clean? I wash him one minute, and he is dirty the minute after." Little Sammy grew frightened and began to cry. "Shut up!" ordered the mother, picking up the child to nurse it again. "Can't you see me take a rest for a minute?"

The hungry child began to cry at the top of its weakened lungs.

"Na, na, you glutton." Hanneh Breineh took out a dirty pacifier from her pocket and stuffed it into the baby's mouth. The grave, pasty-faced infant shrank into a panic of fear, and chewed the nipple nervously, clinging to it with both his thin little hands.

"For what did I need yet the sixth one?" groaned Hanneh Breineh, turning to Mrs. Pelz. "Wasn't it enough five mouths to feed? If I didn't have this child on my neck, I could turn myself around and earn a few cents." She wrung her hands in a passion of despair. "Gottuniu! The earth should only take it before it grows up!"

"Shah! Shah!" reproved Mrs. Pelz. "Pity yourself on the child. Let it grow up already so long as it is here. See how frightened it looks on you." Mrs. Pelz took the child in her arms and petted it. "The poor little lamb! What did it done you should hate it so?"

Hanneh Breineh pushed Mrs. Pelz away from her.

"To whom can I open the wounds of my heart?" she moaned. "Nobody has pity on me. You don't believe me, nobody believes me until I'll fall down like a horse in the middle of the street. Oi weh! Mine life is so black for my eyes! Some mothers got luck. A child gets run over by a car, some fall from a window, some burn themselves up with a match, some get choked with diphtheria; but no death takes mine away."

"God from the world, stop cursing!" admonished Mrs. Pelz. "What do you want from the poor children? Is it their fault that their father makes small wages? Why do you let it all out on them?" Mrs. Pelz sat down beside Hanneh Breineh. "Wait only till your children get old enough to go to the shop and earn money," she consoled. "Push only through those few years while they are yet small; your sun will begin to shine; you will live on the fat of the land, when they begin to bring you in the wages each week."

Hanneh Breineh refused to be comforted.

"Till they are old enough to go to the shop and earn money they'll eat the head off my bones," she wailed. "If you only knew the fights I got by each meal. Maybe I gave Abe a bigger piece of bread than Fanny. Maybe Fanny got a little more soup in her plate than Jake. Eating is dearer than diamonds. Potatoes went up a cent on a pound, and milk is only for millionaires. And once a week, when I buy a little meat for the Sabbath, the butcher weighs it for me like gold, with all the bones in it. When I come to lay the meat out on a plate and divide it up, there ain't nothing to it but bones. Before, he used to throw me in a piece of fat extra or a piece of lung, but now you got to pay for everything, even for a bone to the soup."

"Never mind; you'll yet come out from all your troubles. Just as soon as your children get old enough to get their working papers the more children you got, the more money you'll have."

"Why should I fool myself with the false shine of hope? Don't I know it's already my black luck not to have it good in this world? Do you think American children will right away give everything they earn to their mother?"

"I know what is with you the matter," said Mrs. Pelz. "You didn't eat yet to-day. When it is empty in the stomach, the whole world looks black. Come, only let me give you something good to taste in the mouth; that will freshen you up." Mrs. Pelz went to the cupboard and brought out the saucepan of gefüllte fisch that she had cooked for dinner and placed it on the table in front of Hanneh Breineh. "Give a taste my fish," she said, taking one slice on a spoon, and handing it to Hanneh Breineh with a piece of bread. "I wouldn't give it to you on a plate because I just cleaned up my house, and I don't want to dirty up more dishes."

"What, am I a stranger you should have to serve me on a plate yet!" cried Hanneh Breineh, snatching the fish in her trembling fingers.

"Oi weh! How it melts through all the bones!" she exclaimed, brightening as she ate. "May it be for good luck to us all!" she exulted, waving aloft the last precious bite.

Mrs. Pelz was so flattered that she even ladled up a spoonful of gravy.

"There is a bit of onion and carrot in it," she said, as she handed it to her neighbor.

Hanneh Breineh sipped the gravy drop by drop, like a connoisseur sipping wine.

"Ah-h-h! A taste of that gravy lifts me up to heaven!" As she disposed leisurely of the slice of onion and carrot she relaxed and expanded and even grew jovial. "Let us wish all our troubles on the Russian Czar! Let him burst with our worries for rent! Let him get shriveled with our hunger for bread! Let his eyes dry out of his head looking for work!

"Shah! I'm forgetting from everything," she exclaimed, jumping up. "It must be eleven or soon twelve, and my children will be right away out of school and fall on me like a pack of wild wolves. I better quick run to the market and see what cheaper I can get for a quarter."

Because of the lateness of her coming, the stale bread at the nearest bakeshop was sold out, and Hanneh Breineh had to trudge from shop to shop in search of the usual bargain, and spent nearly an hour to save two cents.

In the meantime the children returned from school, and, finding the door locked, climbed through the fire-escape, and entered the house through the window. Seeing nothing on the table, they rushed to the stove. Abe pulled a steaming potato out of the boiling pot, and so scalded his fingers that the potato fell to the floor, whereupon the three others pounced on it.

"It was my potato," cried Abe, blowing his burned fingers, while with the other hand and his foot he cuffed and kicked the three who were struggling on the floor. A wild fight ensued, and the potato was smashed under Abe's foot amid shouts and screams. Hanneh Breineh, on the stairs, heard the noise of her famished brood, and topped their cries with curses and invective.

"They are here already, the savages! They are here already to shorten my life! They heard you all over the hall, in all the houses around!"

The children, disregarding her words, pounced on her market-basket, shouting ravenously: "Mamma, I'm hungry! What more do you got to eat?"

They tore the bread and herring out of Hanneh Breineh's basket and devoured it in starved savagery, clamoring for more.

"Murderers!" screamed Hanneh Breineh, goaded beyond endurance. "What are you tearing from me my flesh? From where should I steal to give you more? Here I had already a pot of potatoes and a whole loaf of bread and two herrings, and you swallowed it down in the wink of an eye. I have to have Rockefeller's millions to fill your stomachs."

All at once Hanneh Breineh became aware that Benny was missing. "Oi weh!" she burst out, wringing her hands in a new wave of woe, "where is Benny? Didn't he come home yet from school?"

She ran out into the hall, opened the grime-coated window, and looked up and down the street, but Benny was nowhere in sight.

"Abe, Jake, Fanny, quick, find Benny!" entreated Hanneh Breineh, as she rushed back into the kitchen. But the children, anxious to snatch a few minutes' play before the school-call, dodged past her and hurried out.

With the baby on her arm, Hanneh Breineh hastened to the kindergarten.

"Why are you keeping Benny here so long?" she shouted at the teacher as she flung open the door. "If you had my bitter heart, you would send him home long ago and not wait till I got to come for him."

The teacher turned calmly and consulted her record-cards.

"Benny Safron? He wasn't present this morning."

"Not here?" shrieked Hanneh Breineh. "I pushed him out myself he should go. The children didn't want to take him, and I had no time. Woe is me! Where is my child?" She began pulling her hair and beating her breast as she ran into the street.

Mrs. Pelz was busy at a pushcart, picking over some spotted apples, when she heard the clamor of an approaching crowd. A block off she recognized Hanneh Breineh, her hair disheveled, her clothes awry, running toward her with her yelling baby in her arms, the crowd following.

"Friend mine," cried Hanneh Breineh, falling on Mrs. Pelz's neck, "I lost my Benny, the best child of all my children." Tears streamed down her red, swollen eyes as she sobbed. "Benny! mine heart, mine life! Oi-i-i!"

Mrs. Pelz took the frightened baby out of the mother's arms.

"Still yourself a little! See how you're frightening your child."

"Woe to me! Where is my Benny? Maybe he's killed already by a car. Maybe he fainted away from hunger. He didn't eat nothing all day long. Gottuniu! Pity yourself on me!"

She lifted her hands full of tragic entreaty.

"People, my child! Get me my child! I'll go crazy out of my head! Get me my child, or I'll take poison before your eyes!"

"Still yourself a little!" pleaded Mrs. Pelz.

"Talk not to me!" cried Hanneh Breineh, wringing her hands. "You're having all your children. I lost mine. Every good luck comes to other people. But I didn't live yet to see a good day in my life. Mine only joy, mine Benny, is lost away from me."

The crowd followed Hanneh Breineh as she wailed through the street, leaning on Mrs. Pelz. By the time she returned to her house the children were back from school; but seeing that Benny was not there, she chased them out in the street, crying:

"Out of here, you robbers, gluttons! Go find Benny!" Hanneh Breineh crumpled into a chair in utter prostration. "Oi weh! he's lost! Mine life; my little bird; mine only joy! How many nights I spent nursing him when he had the measles! And all that I suffered for weeks and months when he had the whooping-cough! How the eyes went out of my head till I learned him how to walk, till I learned him how to talk! And such a smart child! If I lost all the others, it wouldn't tear me so by the heart."

She worked herself up into such a hysteria, crying, and tearing her hair, and hitting her head with her knuckles, that at last she fell into a faint. It took some time before Mrs. Pelz, with the aid of neighbors, revived her.

"Benny, mine angel!" she moaned as she opened her eyes.

Just then a policeman came in with the lost Benny.

"Na, na, here you got him already!" said Mrs. Pelz. "Why did you carry on so for nothing? Why did you tear up the world like a crazy?"

The child's face was streaked with tears as he cowered, frightened and forlorn. Hanneh Breineh sprang toward him, slapping his cheeks, boxing his ears, before the neighbors could rescue him from her.

"Woe on your head!" cried the mother. "Where did you lost yourself? Ain't I got enough worries on my head than to go around looking for you? I didn't have yet a minute's peace from that child since he was born!"

"See a crazy mother!" remonstrated Mrs. Pelz, rescuing Benny from another beating. "Such a mouth! With one breath she blesses him when he is lost, and with the other breath she curses him when he is found."

Hanneh Breineh took from the windowsill a piece of herring covered with swarming flies, and putting it on a slice of dry bread, she filled a cup of tea that had been stewing all day, and dragged Benny over to the table to eat.

But the child, choking with tears, was unable to touch the food.

"Go eat!" commanded Hanneh Breineh. "Eat and choke yourself eating!"

"Maybe she won't remember me no more. Maybe the servant won't let me in," thought Mrs. Pelz, as she walked by the brownstone house on Eighty-Fourth Street where she had been told Hanneh Breineh now lived. At last she summoned up enough courage to climb the steps. She was all out of breath as she rang the bell with trembling fingers. "Oi weh! even the outside smells riches and plenty! Such curtains! And shades on all windows like by millionaires! Twenty years ago she used to eat from the pot to the hand, and now she lives in such a palace."

A whiff of steam-heated warmth swept over Mrs. Pelz as the door opened, and she saw her old friend of the tenements dressed in silk and diamonds like a being from another world.

"Mrs. Pelz, is it you!" cried Hanneh Breineh, overjoyed at the sight of her former neighbor. "Come right in. Since when are you back in New York?"

"We came last week," mumbled Mrs. Pelz, as she was led into a richly carpeted reception-room.

"Make yourself comfortable. Take off your shawl," urged Hanneh Breineh.

But Mrs. Pelz only drew her shawl more tightly around her, a keen sense of her poverty gripping her as she gazed, abashed by the luxurious wealth that shone from every corner.

"This shawl covers up my rags," she said, trying to hide her shabby sweater.

"I'll tell you what; come right into the kitchen," suggested Hanneh Breineh. "The servant is away for this afternoon, and we can feel more comfortable there. I can breathe like a free person in my kitchen when the girl has her day out."

Mrs. Pelz glanced about her in an excited daze. Never in her life had she seen anything so wonderful as a white-tiled kitchen, with its glistening porcelain sink and the aluminum pots and pans that shone like silver.

"Where are you staying now?" asked Hanneh Breineh, as she pinned an apron over her silk dress.

"I moved back to Delancey Street, where we used to live," replied Mrs. Pelz, as she seated herself cautiously in a white enameled chair.

"Oi weh! What grand times we had in that old house when we were neighbors!" sighed Hanneh Breineh, looking at her old friend with misty eyes.

"You still think on Delancey Street? Haven't you more high-class neighbors uptown here?"

"A good neighbor is not to be found every day," deplored Hanneh Breineh. "Uptown here, where each lives in his own house, nobody cares if the person next door is dying or going crazy from loneliness. It ain't anything like we used to have it in Delancey Street, when we could walk into one another's rooms without knocking, and borrow a pinch of salt or a pot to cook in."

Hanneh Breineh went over to the pantry-shelf.

"We are going to have a bite right here on the kitchen-table like on Delancey Street. So long there's no servant to watch us we can eat what we please."

"Oi! How it waters my mouth with appetite, the smell of the herring and onion!" chuckled Mrs. Pelz, sniffing the welcome odors with greedy pleasure.

Hanneh Breineh pulled a dishtowel from the rack and threw one end of it to Mrs. Pelz.

"So long there's no servant around, we can use it together for a napkin. It's dirty, anyhow. How it freshens up my heart to see you!" she rejoiced as she poured out her tea into a saucer. "If you would only know how I used to beg my daughter to write for me a letter to you; but these American children, what is to them a mother's feelings?"

"What are you talking!" cried Mrs. Pelz. "The whole world rings with you and your children. Everybody is envying you. Tell me how began your luck?"

"You heard how my husband died with consumption," replied Hanneh Breineh. "The five hundred dollars lodge money gave me the first lift in life, and I opened a little grocery store. Then my son Abe married himself to a girl with a thousand dollars. That started him in business, and now he has the biggest shirtwaist factory on West Twenty-Ninth Street."

"Yes, I heard your son had a factory." Mrs. Pelz hesitated and stammered; "I'll tell you the truth. What I came to ask you—I thought maybe you would beg your son Abe if he would give my husband a job."

"Why not?" said Hanneh Breineh. "He keeps more than five hundred hands. I'll ask him if he should take in Mr. Pelz."

"Long years on you, Hanneh Breineh! You'll save my life if you could only help my husband get work."

"Of course my son will help him. All my children like to do good. My daughter Fanny is a milliner on Fifth Avenue, and she takes in the poorest girls in her shop and even pays them sometimes while they learn the trade." Hanneh Breineh's face lit up, and her chest filled with pride as she enumerated the successes of her children. "And my son Benny he wrote a play on Broadway, and he gave away more than a hundred free tickets for the first night."

"Benny? The one who used to get lost from home all the time? You always did love that child more than all the rest. And what is Sammy your baby doing?"

"He ain't a baby no longer. He goes to college and quarterbacks the football team. They can't get along without him.

"And my son Jake, I nearly forgot him. He began collecting rent in Delancey Street, and now he is boss of renting the swellest apartmenthouses on Riverside Drive."

"What did I tell you? In America children are like money in the bank," purred Mrs. Pelz, as she pinched and patted Hanneh Breineh's silk sleeve. "Oi weh! How it shines from you! You ought to kiss the air and dance for joy and happiness. It is such a bitter frost outside; a pail of coal is so dear, and you got it so warm with steam heat. I had to pawn my feather bed to have enough for the rent, and you are rolling in money."

"Yes, I got it good in some ways, but money ain't everything," sighed Hanneh Breineh.

"You ain't yet satisfied?"

"But here I got no friends," complained Hanneh Breineh.

"Friends?" queried Mrs. Pelz. "What greater friend is there on earth than the dollar?"

"Oi! Mrs. Pelz; if you could only look into my heart! I'm so choked up! You know they say a cow has a long tongue, but can't talk." Hanneh Breineh shook her head wistfully, and her eyes filmed with inward brooding. "My children give me everything from the best. When I was sick, they got me a nurse by day and one by night. They bought me the best wine. If I asked for dove's milk, they would buy it for me; but—but—I can't talk myself out in their language. They want to make me over for an American lady, and I'm different." Tears cut their way under her eyelids with a pricking pain as she went on: "When I was poor, I was free, and could holler and do what I like in my own house. Here I got to lie still like a mouse under a broom. Between living up to my Fifth-Avenue daughter and keeping up with the servants, I am like a sinner in the next world that is thrown from one hell to another." The doorbell rang, and Hanneh Breineh jumped up with a start.

"Oi weh! It must be the servant back already!" she exclaimed, as she tore off her apron. "Oi weh! Let's quickly put the dishes together in a dishpan. If she sees I eat on the kitchen table, she will look on me like the dirt under her feet."

Mrs. Pelz seized her shawl in haste.

"I better run home quick in my rags before your servant sees me."

"I'll speak to Abe about the job," said Hanneh Breineh, as she pushed a bill into the hand of Mrs. Pelz, who edged out as the servant entered.

"I'm having fried potato lotkes special for you, Benny," said Hanneh Breineh, as the children gathered about the table for the family dinner given in honor of Benny's success with his new play. "Do you remember how you used to lick the fingers from them?"

"Oh, mother!" reproved Fanny. "Any one hearing you would think we were still in the pushcart district."

"Stop your nagging, sis, and let ma alone," commanded Benny, patting his mother's arm affectionately. "I'm home only once a month. Let her feed me what she pleases. My stomach is bomb-proof."

"Do I hear that the President is coming to your play?" said Abe, as he stuffed a napkin over his diamond-studded shirt-front.

"Why shouldn't he come?" returned Benny. "The critics say it's the greatest antidote for the race hatred created by the war. If you want to know, he is coming tonight; and what's more, our box is next to the President's."

"Nu, mammeh," sallied Jake, "did you ever dream in Delancey Street that we should rub sleeves with the President?"

"I always said that Benny had more head than the rest of you," replied the mother.

As the laughter died away, Jake went on:

"Honor you are getting plenty; but how much mezummmen does this play bring you? Can I invest any of it in real estate for you?"

"I'm getting ten per cent royalties of the gross receipts," replied the youthful playwright.

"How much is that?" queried Hanneh Breineh.

"Enough to buy up all your fish-markets in Delancey Street," laughed Abe in good-natured raillery at his mother.

Her son's jest cut like a knife-thrust in her heart. She felt her heart ache with the pain that she was shut out from their successes. Each added triumph only widened the gulf. And when she tried to bridge this gulf by asking questions, they only thrust her back upon herself.

"Your fame has even helped me get my hat trade

solid with the Four Hundred," put in Fanny. "You bet I let Mrs. Van Suyden know that our box is next to the President's. She said she would drop in to meet you. Of course she let on to me that she hadn't seen the play yet, though my designer said she saw her there on the opening night."

"Oh, Gosh, the toadies!" sneered Benny. "Nothing so sickens you with success as the way people who once shoved you off the sidewalk come crawling to you on their stomachs begging you to dine with them."

"Say, that leading man of yours he's some class!" cried Fanny. "That's the man I'm looking for. Will you invite him to supper after the theater?"

The playwright turned to his mother.

"Say, ma," he said laughingly, "how would you like a real actor for a son-in-law?"

"She should worry," mocked Sam. "She'll be discussing with him the future of the Greek drama. Too bad it doesn't happen to be Warfield, or mother could give him tips on the 'Auctioneer.'"

Jake turned to his mother with a covert grin.

"I guess you'd have no objection if Fanny got next to Benny's leading man. He makes at least fifteen hundred a week. That wouldn't be such a bad addition to the family, would it?"

Again the bantering tone stabbed Hanneh Breineh. Everything in her began to tremble and break loose.

"Why do you ask me?" she cried, throwing her napkin into her plate. "Do I count for a person in this house? If I'll say something, will you even listen to me? What is to me the grandest man that my daughter could pick out? Another enemy in my house! Another person to shame himself from me!" She swept in her children in one glance of despairing anguish as she rose from the table. "What worth is an old mother to American children? The President is coming tonight to the theater, and none of you asked me to go." Unable to check the rising tears, she fled toward the kitchen and banged the door.

They all looked at one another guiltily.

"Say, sis," Benny called out sharply, "what sort of frame-up is this? Haven't you told mother that she was to go with us tonight?"

"Yes—I—" Fanny bit her lips as she fumbled evasively for words. "I asked her if she wouldn't mind my taking her some other time."

"Now you have made a mess of it!" fumed Benny. "Mother'll be too hurt to go now."

"Well, I don't care," snapped Fanny. "I can't appear with mother in a box at the theater. Can I introduce her to Mrs. Van Suyden? And suppose your leading man should ask to meet me?"

"Take your time, sis. He hasn't asked yet," scoffed Benny.

"The more reason I shouldn't spoil my chances. You know mother. She'll spill the beans that we come from Delancey Street the minute we introduce her anywhere. Must I always have the black shadow of my past trailing after me?"

"But have you no feelings for mother?" admonished Abe.

"I've tried harder than all of you to do my duty. I've *lived* with her." She turned angrily upon them. "I've borne the shame of mother while you bought her off with a present and a treat here and there. God knows how hard I tried to civilize her so as not to have to blush with shame when I take her anywhere. I dressed her in the most stylish Paris models, but Delancey Street sticks out from every inch of her. Whenever she opens her mouth, I'm done for. You fellows had your chance to rise in the world because a man is free to go up as high as he can reach up to; but I, with all my style and pep, can't get a man my equal because a girl is always judged by her mother."

They were silenced by her vehemence, and unconsciously turned to Benny.

"I guess we all tried to do our best for mother," said Benny, thoughtfully. "But wherever there is growth, there is pain and heartbreak. The trouble with us is that the ghetto of the Middle Ages and the children of the twentieth century have to live under one roof, and—"

A sound of crashing dishes came from the kitchen, and the voice of Hanneh Breineh resounded through the diningroom as she wreaked her pent-up fury on the helpless servant.

"Oh, my nerves! I can't stand it any more! There will be no girl again for another week!" cried Fanny.

"Oh, let up on the old lady," protested Abe. "Since she can't take it out on us any more, what harm is it if she cusses the servants?"

"If you fellows had to chase around employment agencies, you wouldn't see anything funny about it. Why can't we move into a hotel that will do away with the need of servants altogether?"

"I got it better," said Jake, consulting a notebook from his pocket. "I have on my list an apartment on Riverside Drive where there's only a small kitchenette; but we can do away with the cooking, for there is a dining service in the building."

The new Riverside apartment to which Hanneh Breineh was removed by her socially ambitious children was for the habitually active mother an empty desert of enforced idleness. Deprived of her kitchen, Hanneh Breineh felt robbed of the last reason for her existence. Cooking and marketing and puttering busily with pots and pans gave her an excuse for living and struggling and bearing up with her children. The lonely idleness of Riverside Drive stunned all her senses and arrested all her thoughts. It gave her that choked sense of being cut off from air, from life, from everything warm and human. The cold indifference, the each-for-himself look in the eyes of the people about her were like stinging slaps in the face. Even the children had nothing real or human in them. They were starched and stiff miniatures of their elders.

But the most unendurable part of the stifling life on Riverside Drive was being forced to eat in the public diningroom. No matter how hard she tried to learn polite table manners, she always found people staring at her, and her daughter rebuking her for eating with the wrong fork or guzzling the soup or staining the cloth.

In a fit of rebellion Hanneh Breineh resolved never to go down to the public diningroom again, but to make use of the gas-stove in the kitchenette to cook her own meals. That very day she rode down to Delancey Street and purchased a new market-basket. For some time she walked among the haggling pushcart venders, relaxing and swimming in the warm waves of her old familiar past.

A fish-peddler held up a large carp in his black, hairy hand and waved it dramatically:

"Women! Women! Fourteen cents a pound!"

He ceased his raucous shouting as he saw Hanneh Breineh in her rich attire approach his cart.

"How much?" she asked, pointing to the fattest carp.

"Fifteen cents, lady," said the peddler, smirking as he raised his price.

"Swindler! Didn't I hear you call fourteen cents?" shrieked Hanneh Breineh, exultingly, the spirit of the penny chase surging in her blood. Diplomatically, Hanneh Breineh turned as if to go, and the fisherman seized her basket in frantic fear.

"I should live; I'm losing money on the fish, lady," whined the peddler. "I'll let it down to thirteen cents for you only."

"Two pounds for a quarter, and not a penny more," said Hanneh Breineh, thrilling again with the rare sport of bargaining, which had been her chief joy in the good old days of poverty.

"Nu, I want to make the first sale for good luck." The peddler threw the fish on the scale.

As he wrapped up the fish, Hanneh Breineh saw the driven look of worry in his haggard eyes, and when he counted out the change from her dollar, she waved it aside. "Keep it for your luck," she said, and hurried off to strike a new bargain at a pushcart of onions.

Hanneh Breineh returned triumphantly with her purchases. The basket under her arm gave forth the old, homelike odors of herring and garlic, while the scaly tail of a four-pound carp protruded from its newspaper wrapping. A gilded placard on the door of the apartment-house proclaimed that all merchandise must be delivered through the trade entrance in the rear; but Hanneh Breineh with her basket strode proudly through the marble-paneled hall and rang nonchalantly for the elevator.

The uniformed hall-man, erect, expressionless, frigid with dignity, stepped forward:

"Just a minute, madam. I'll call a boy to take up your basket for you."

Hanneh Breineh, glaring at him, jerked the basket savagely from his hands. "Mind your own business!" she retorted. "I'll take it up myself. Do you think you're a Russian policeman to boss me in my own house?"

Angry lines appeared on the countenance of the representative of social decorum.

"It is against the rules, madam," he said, stiffly.

"You should sink into the earth with all your rules and brass buttons. Ain't this America? Ain't this a free country? Can't I take up in my own house what I buy with my own money?" cried Hanneh Breineh, reveling in the opportunity to shower forth the volley of invectives that had been suppressed in her for the weeks of deadly dignity of Riverside Drive.

In the midst of this uproar Fanny came in with Mrs. Van Suyden. Hanneh Breineh rushed over to her, crying:

"This bossy policeman won't let me take up my basket in the elevator."

The daughter, unnerved with shame and confusion, took the basket in her white-gloved hand and ordered the hall-boy to take it around to the regular delivery entrance.

Hanneh Breineh was so hurt by her daughter's apparent defense of the hall-man's rules that she utterly ignored Mrs. Van Suyden's greeting and walked up the seven flights of stairs out of sheer spite.

"You see the tragedy of my life?" broke out Fanny, turning to Mrs. Van Suyden.

"You poor child! You go right up to your dear, old lady mother, and I'll come some other time."

Instantly Fanny regretted her words. Mrs. Van Suyden's pity only roused her wrath the more against her mother.

Breathless from climbing the stairs, Hanneh Brei-

neh entered the apartment just as Fanny tore the fault-
less millinery creation from her head and threw it on the
floor in a rage.

"Mother, you are the ruination of my life! You have
driven away Mrs. Van Suyden, as you have driven away
all my best friends. What do you think we got this apartment for but to get rid of your fish smells and your
brawls with the servants? And here you come with a
basket on your arm as if you just landed from steerage!
And this afternoon, of all times, when Benny is bringing
his leading man to tea. When will you ever stop dis-
gracing us?"

"When I'm dead," said Hanneh Breineh, grimly.
"When the earth will cover me up, then you'll be free
to go your American way. I'm not going to make myself
over for a lady on Riverside Drive. I hate you and all
your swell friends. I'll not let myself be choked up here
by you or by that hall-boss policeman that is higher in
your eyes than your own mother."

"So that's your thanks for all we've done for you?"
cried the daughter.

"All you've done for me!" shouted Hanneh Breineh.
"What have you done for me? You hold me like a dog
on a chain! It stands in the Talmud; some children give
their mothers dry bread and water and go to heaven
for it, and some give their mother roast duck and go to
Gehenna because it's not given with love."

"You want me to love you yet? raged the daughter.
"You knocked every bit of love out of me when I was yet
a kid. All the memories of childhood I have is your everlasting cursing and yelling that we were gluttons."

The bell rang sharply, and Hanneh Breineh flung
open the door.

"Your groceries, ma'am," said the boy.

Hanneh Breineh seized the basket from him, and with a vicious fling sent it rolling across the room, strewing its contents over the Persian rugs and inlaid floor. Then seizing her hat and coat, she stormed out of the apartment and down the stairs.

Mr. and Mrs. Pelz sat crouched and shivering over their meager supper when the door opened, and Hanneh Breineh in fur coat and plumed hat charged into the room.

"I come to cry out to you my bitter heart," she sobbed. "Woe is me! It is so black for my eyes!"

"What is the matter with you, Hanneh Breineh?" cried Mrs. Pelz in bewildered alarm.

"I am turned out of my own house by the brass-buttoned policeman that bosses the elevator. Oi-i-i-i! Weh-h-h-h! What have I from my life? The whole world rings with my son's play. Even the President came to see it, and I, his mother, have not seen it yet. My heart is dying in me like in a prison," she went on wailing. "I am starved out for a piece of real eating. In that swell restaurant is nothing but napkins and forks and lettuce-leaves. There are a dozen plates to every bite of food. And it looks so fancy on the plate, but it's nothing but straw in the mouth. I'm starving, but I can't swallow down their American eating."

"Hanneh Breineh," said Mrs. Pelz, "you are sinning before God. Look on your fur coat; it alone would feed a whole family for a year. I never had yet a piece of fur trimming on a coat, and you are in fur from the neck to the feet. I never had yet a piece of feather on a hat, and your hat is all feathers."

"What are you envying me?" protested Hanneh Breineh. "What have I from all my fine furs and feathers when my children are strangers to me? All the fur coats in the world can't warm up the loneliness inside my heart. All the grandest feathers can't hide the bitter shame in my face that my children shame themselves from me."

Hanneh Breineh suddenly loomed over them like some ancient, heroic figure of the Bible condemning unrighteousness.

"Why should my children shame themselves from me? From where did they get the stuff to work themselves up in the world? Did they get it from the air? How did they get all their smartness to rise over the people around them? Why don't the children of born American mothers write my Benny's plays? It is I, who never had a chance to be a person, who gave him the fire in his head. If I would have had a chance to go to school and learn the language, what couldn't I have been? It is I and my mother and my mother's mother and my father and father's father who had such a black life in Poland; it is our choked thoughts and feelings that are flaming up in my children and making them great in America. And yet they shame themselves from me!"

For a moment Mr. and Mrs. Pelz were hypnotized by the sweep of her words. Then Hanneh Breineh sank into a chair in utter exhaustion. She began to weep bitterly, her body shaking with sobs.

"Woe is me! For what did I suffer and hope on my children? A bitter old age—my end. I'm so lonely!"

All the dramatic fire seemed to have left her. The spell was broken. They saw the Hanneh Breineh of old, ever discontented, ever complaining even in the midst of riches and plenty.

"Hanneh Breineh," said Mrs. Pelz, "the only trouble with you is that you got it too good. People will tear the eyes out of your head because you're complaining yet. If

I only had your fur coat! If I only had your diamonds! I have nothing. You have everything. You are living on the fat of the land. You go right back home and thank God that you don't have my bitter lot."

"You got to let me stay here with you," insisted Hanneh Breineh. "I'll not go back to my children except when they bury me. When they will see my dead face, they will understand how they killed me."

Mrs. Pelz glanced nervously at her husband. They barely had enough covering for their one bed; how could they possibly lodge a visitor?

"I don't want to take up your bed," said Hanneh Breineh. "I don't care if I have to sleep on the floor or on the chairs, but I'll stay here for the night."

Seeing that she was bent on staying, Mr. Pelz prepared to sleep by putting a few chairs next to the trunk, and Hanneh Breineh was invited to share the rickety bed with Mrs. Pelz.

The mattress was full of lumps and hollows. Hanneh Breineh lay cramped and miserable, unable to stretch out her limbs. For years she had been accustomed to hair mattresses and ample woolen blankets, so that though she covered herself with her fur coat, she was too cold to sleep. But worse than the cold were the creeping things on the wall. And as the lights were turned low, the mice came through the broken plaster and raced across the floor. The foul odors of the kitchen-sink added to the night of horrors.

"Are you going back home?" asked Mrs. Pelz, as Hanneh Breineh put on her hat and coat the next morning.

"I don't know where I'm going," she replied, as she put a bill into Mrs. Pelz's hand.

For hours Hanneh Breineh walked through the

crowded ghetto streets. She realized that she no longer could endure the sordid ugliness of her past, and yet she could not go home to her children. She only felt that she must go on and on.

In the afternoon a cold, drizzling rain set in. She was worn out from the sleepless night and hours of tramping. With a piercing pain in her heart she at last turned back and boarded the subway for Riverside Drive. She had fled from the marble sepulcher of the Riverside apartment to her old home in the ghetto; but now she knew that she could not live there again. She had outgrown her past by the habits of years of physical comforts, and these material comforts that she could no longer do without choked and crushed the life within her.

A cold shudder went through Hanneh Breineh as she approached the apartment-house. Peering through the plate glass of the door she saw the face of the uniformed hallman. For a hesitating moment she remained standing in the drizzling rain, unable to enter, and yet knowing full well that she would have to enter.

Then suddenly Hanneh Breineh began to laugh. She realized that it was the first time she had laughed since her children had become rich. But it was the hard laugh of bitter sorrow. Tears streamed down her furrowed cheeks as she walked slowly up the granite steps.

"The fat of the land!" muttered Hanneh Breineh, with a choking sob as the hall-man with immobile face deferentially swung open the door—"the fat of the land!"

The Lost "Beautifulness"

"OI, WEH! How it shines the beautifulness!" exulted Hanneh Hayyeh over her newly painted kitchen. She cast a glance full of worship and adoration at the picture of her son in uniform; eyes like her own, shining with eagerness, with joy of life, looked back at her.

"Aby will not have to shame himself to come back to his old home," she rejoiced, clapping her hands— hands blistered from the paintbrush and calloused from rough toil. "Now he'll be able to invite all the grandest friends he made in the army."

The smell of the paint was suffocating, but she inhaled in it huge draughts of hidden beauty. For weeks she had dreamed of it and felt in each tin of paint she was able to buy, in each stroke of the brush, the ecstasy of loving service for the son she idolized.

Ever since she first began to wash the fine silks and linens for Mrs. Preston, years ago, it had been Hanneh Hayyeh's ambition to have a white-painted kitchen exactly like that in the old Stuyvesant Square mansion. Now her own kitchen was a dream come true.

Hanneh Hayyeh ran in to her husband, a stoop-shouldered, care-crushed man who was leaning against the bed, his swollen feet out-stretched, counting the pennies that totaled his day's earnings.

"Jake Safransky!" she cried excitedly, "you got to come in and give a look on my painting before you go to sleep."

"Oi, let me alone. Give me only a rest."

Too intoxicated with the joy of achievement to take no for an answer, she dragged him into the doorway.

"Nu? How do you like it? Do I know what beautiful is?"

"But how much money did you spend out on that paint?"

"It was my own money," she said, wiping the perspiration off her face with a corner of her apron. "Every penny I earned myself from the extra washing."

"But you had ought save it up for the bad times. What'll you do when the cold weather starts in and the pushcart will not wheel itself out?"

"I save and pinch enough for myself. This I done in honor for my son. I want my Aby to lift up his head in the world. I want him to be able to invite even the President from America to his home and shame himself."

"You'd pull the bananas off a blind man's pushcart to bring to your Aby. You know nothing from holding tight to a dollar and saving a penny to a penny like poor people should."

"What do I got from living if I can't have a little beautifulness in my life? I don't allow for myself the ten cents to go to a moving picture that I'm crazy to see. I never yet treated myself to an ice-cream soda even for a holiday. Shining up the house for Aby is my only pleasure."

"Yah, but it ain't your house. It's the landlord's."

"Don't I live in it? I soak in pleasure from every inch of my kitchen. Why, I could kiss the grand white color on the walls. It lights up my eyes like sunshine in the room."

Her glance traveled from the newly painted walls to the geranium on the window-sill, and back to her husband's face.

"Jake!" she cried, shaking him, "ain't you got eyes? How can you look on the way it dances the beautifulness from every corner and not jump in the air from happiness?"

"I'm only thinking on the money you spent out on the landlord's house. Look only on me! I'm black from worry, but no care lays on your head. It only dreams itself in you how to make yourself for an American and lay in every penny you got on fixing out the house like the rich."

"I'm sick of living like a pig with my nose to the earth, all the time only pinching and scraping for bread and rent. So long my Aby is with America, I want to make myself for an American. I could tear the stars out from heaven for my Aby's wish."

Her sunken cheeks were flushed and her eyes glowed with light as she gazed about her.

"When I see myself around the house how I fixed it up with my own hands, I forget I'm only a nobody. It makes me feel I'm also a person like Mrs. Preston. It lifts me with high thoughts."

"Why didn't you marry yourself to a millionaire? You always want to make yourself like Mrs. Preston who got millions laying in the bank."

"But Mrs. Preston does make me feel that I'm alike with her," returned Hanneh Hayyeh, proudly. "Don't she talk herself out to me like I was her friend? Mrs. Preston says this war is to give everybody a chance to lift up his head like a person. It is to bring together the people on top who got everything and the people on the bottom who got nothing. She's been telling me about a new word—democracy. It got me on fire. Democracy means that everybody in America is going to be with everybody alike."

"Och! Stop your dreaming out of your head. Close up your mouth from your foolishness. Women got long hair and small brains," he finished, muttering as he went to bed.

At the busy gossiping hour of the following morning

when the butcher-shop was crowded with women in dressing-sacks and wrappers covered over with shawls, Hanneh Hayyeh elbowed her way into the clamorous babel of her neighbors.

"What are you so burning? What are you so flaming?"

"She's always on fire with the wonders of her son."

"The whole world must stop still to listen to what news her son writes to her."

"She thinks her son is the only one soldier by the American army."

"My Benny is also one great wonder from smartness, but I ain't such a crazy mother like she."

The voices of her neighbors rose from every corner, but Hanneh Hayyeh, deaf to all, projected herself forward.

"What are you pushing yourself so wild? You ain't going to get your meat first. Ain't it, Mr. Sopkin, all got to wait their turn?"

Mr. Sopkin glanced up in the midst of cutting apart a quarter of meat. He wiped his knife on his greasy apron and leaned across the counter.

"Nu? Hannah Hayyeh?" his ruddy face beamed. "Have you another letter from little Aby in France? What good news have you got to tell us?"

"No—it's not a letter," she retorted, with a gesture of impatience. "The good news is that I got done with the painting of my kitchen—and you all got to come and give a look how it shines in my house like in a palace."

Mr. Sopkin resumed cutting the meat.

"Oi weh!" clamored Hanneh Hayyeh, with feverish breathlessness. "Stop with your meat already and quick come. The store ain't going to run away from you! It will take only a minute. With one step you are upstairs in my house." She flung out her hands. "And everybody got to come along."

"Do you think I can make a living from looking on the wonders you turn over in your house?" remonstrated the butcher, with a twinkle in his eye.

"Making money ain't everything in life. My new-painted kitchen will light up your heart with joy."

Seeing that Mr. Sopkin still made no move, she began to coax and wheedle, woman-fashion. "Oi weh! Mr. Sopkin! Don't be so mean. Come only. Your customers ain't going to run away from you. If they do, they only got to come back, because you ain't a skinner. You weigh the meat honest."

How could Mr. Sopkin resist such seductive flattery?

"Hanneh Hayyeh!" he laughed. "You're crazy up in the air, but nobody can say no to anything you take into your head."

He tossed his knife down on the counter. "Everybody!" he called; "let us do her the pleasure and give a look on what she got to show us."

"Oi weh! I ain't got no time," protested one. "I left my baby alone in the house locked in."

"And I left a pot of eating on the stove boiling. It must be all burned away by this time."

"But you all got time to stand around here and chatter like a box of monkeys, for hours," admonished Mr. Sopkin. "This will only take a minute. You know Hanneh Hayyeh. We can't tear ourselves away from her till we do what wills itself in her mind."

Protesting and gesticulating, they all followed Mr. Sopkin as Hanneh Hayyeh led the way. Through the hallway of a dark, ill-smelling tenement, up two flights of crooked, rickety stairs, they filed. When Hanneh Hayyeh opened the door there were exclamations of wonder and joy: "Oi! Oi!" and "Ay! Ay! Takeh! Takeh!

"Gold is shining from every corner!"

"Like for a holiday!"

"You don't need to light up the gas, so it shines!"

"I wish I could only have it so grand!"

"You ain't got worries on your head, so it lays in your mind to make it so fancy."

Mr. Sopkin stood with mouth open, stunned with wonder at the transformation.

Hanneh Hayyeh shook him by the sleeve exultantly. "Nu? Why ain't you saying something?"

"Grand ain't the word for it! What a whiteness! And what a cleanliness! It tears out the eyes from the head! Such a tenant the landlord ought to give out a medal or let down the rent free. I saw the rooms before and I see them now. What a difference from one house to another."

"Ain't you coming in?" Hanneh Hayyeh besought her neighbors.

"God from the world! To step with our feet on this new painted floor?"

"Shah!" said the butcher, taking off his apron and spreading it on the floor. "You can all give a step on my apron. It's dirty, anyhow."

They crowded in on the outspread apron and vied with one another in their words of praise.

"May you live to see your son married from this kitchen, and may we all be invited to the wedding!"

"May you live to eat here cake and wine on the feasts of your grandchildren!"

"May you have the luck to get rich and move from here into your own bought house!"

"Amen!" breathed Hanneh Hayyeh. "May we all forget from our worries for rent!"

Mrs. Preston followed with keen delight Hanneh Hayyeh's every movement as she lifted the wash from the basket and spread it on the bed. Hanneh Hayyeh's rough, toil-worn hands lingered lovingly, caressingly over each garment. It was as though the fabrics held something subtly animate in their texture that penetrated to her very finger-tips.

"Hanneh Hayyeh! You're an artist!" There was reverence in Mrs. Preston's low voice that pierced the other woman's inmost being. "You do my laces and batistes as no one else ever has. It's as if you breathed part of your soul into it."

The hungry-eyed, ghetto woman drank in thirstily the beauty and goodness that radiated from Mrs. Preston's person. None of the cultured elegance of her adored friend escaped Hanneh Hayyeh. Her glance traveled from the exquisite shoes to the flawless hair of the well-poised head.

"Your things got so much fineness. I'm crazy for the feel from them. I do them up so light in my hands like it was thin air I was handling."

Hanneh Hayyeh pantomimed as she spoke and Mrs. Preston, roused from her habitual reserve, put her fine, white hand affectionately over Hanneh Hayyeh's gnarled, roughened ones.

"Oi-i-i-i! Mrs. Preston! You always make me feel so grand!" said Hanneh Hayyeh, a mist of tears in her wistful eyes. "When I go away from you I could just sit down and cry. I can't give it out in words what it is. It chokes me so—how good you are to me—You ain't at all like a rich lady. You're so plain from the heart. You make the lowest nobody feel he's somebody."

"You are not a 'nobody,' Hanneh Hayyeh. You are an artist—an artist laundress."

"What mean you an artist?"

"An artist is so filled with love for the beautiful that

he has to express it in some way. You express it in your washing just as a painter paints it in a picture."

"Paint?" exclaimed Hanneh Hayyeh. "If you could only give a look how I painted up my kitchen! It lights up the whole tenement house for blocks around. The grocer and the butcher and all the neighbors were jumping in the air from wonder and joy when they seen how I shined up my house."

"And all in honor of Aby's home-coming?" Mrs. Preston smiled, her thoughts for a moment on her own son, the youngest captain in his regiment whose homecoming had been delayed from week to week.

"Everything I do is done for my Aby," breathed Hanneh Hayyeh, her hands clasping her bosom as if feeling again the throb of his babyhood at her heart. "But this painting was already dreaming itself in my head for years. You remember the time the hot iron fell on my foot and you came to see me and brought me a red flower-pot wrapped around with green crepe paper? That flower-pot opened up the sky in my kitchen." The words surged from the seething soul of her. "Right away I saw before my eyes how I could shine up my kitchen like a parlor by painting the walls and sewing up new curtains for the window. It was like seeing before me your face every time I looked on your flowers. I used to talk to it like it could hear and feel and see. And I said to it: 'I'll show you what's in me. I'll show you that I know what beautiful is.'"

Her face was aglow with an enthusiasm that made it seem young, like a young girl's face.

"I begged myself by the landlord to paint up my kitchen, but he wouldn't listen to me. So I seen that if I ever hoped to fix up my house, I'd have to spend out my own money. And I began to save a penny to a penny to have for the paint. And when I seen the painters, I always stopped them to ask where and how to buy it so that it should come out the cheapest. By day and by night it burned in me the picture—my kitchen shining all white like yours, till I couldn't rest till I done it."

With all her breeding, with all the restraint of her Anglo-Saxon forbears, Mrs. Preston was strangely shaken by Hanneh Hayyeh's consuming passion for beauty. She looked deep into the eyes of the Russian Jewess as if drinking in the secret of their hidden glow.

"I am eager to see that wonderful kitchen of yours," she said, as Hanneh Hayyeh bade her good-bye.

Hanneh Hayyeh walked home, her thoughts in a whirl with the glad anticipation of Mrs. Preston's promised visit. She wondered how she might share the joy of Mrs. Preston's presence with the butcher and all the neighbors. "I'll bake up a shtrudel cake," she thought to herself. "They will all want to come to get a taste of the cake and then they'll give a look on Mrs. Preston."

Thus smiling and talking to herself she went about her work. As she bent over the wash-tub rubbing the clothes, she visualized the hot, steaming shtrudel just out of the oven and the exclamations of pleasure as Mrs. Preston and the neighbors tasted it. All at once there was a knock at the door. Wiping her soapy hands on the corner of her apron, she hastened to open it.

"Oi! Mr. Landlord! Come only inside," she urged. "I got the rent for you, but I want you to give a look around how I shined up my flat."

The Prince Albert that bound the protruding stomach of Mr. Benjamin Rosenblatt was no tighter than the skin that encased the smooth-shaven face. His mouth was tight. Even the small, popping eyes held a tight gleam.

"I got no time. The minutes is money," he said, extending a claw-like hand for the rent.

"But I only want you for a half a minute." And Hanneh Hayyeh dragged the owner of her palace across the threshold. "Nu? Ain't I a good painter? And all this I done while other people were sleeping themselves, after I'd come home from my day's work."

"Very nice," condescended Mr. Benjamin Rosenblatt, with a hasty glance around the room. "You certainly done a good job. But I got to go. Here's your receipt." And the fingers that seized Hanneh Hayyeh's rent-money seemed like pincers for grasping molars.

Two weeks later Jake Safransky and his wife Hanneh Hayyeh sat eating their dinner, when the janitor came in with a note.

"From the landlord," he said, handing it to Hanneh Hayyeh, and walked out.

"The landlord?" she cried, excitedly. "What for can it be?" With trembling fingers she tore open the note. The slip dropped from her hand. Her face grew livid, her eyes bulged with terror. "Oi weh!" she exclaimed, as she fell back against the wall.

"Gewalt!" cried her husband, seizing her limp hand, "you look like struck dead."

"Oi-i-i! The murderer! He raised me the rent five dollars a month."

"Good for you! I told you to listen to me. Maybe he thinks we got money laying in the bank when you got so many dollars to give out on paint."

She turned savagely on her husband. "What are you tearing yet my flesh? Such a money-grabber! How could I imagine for myself that so he would thank me for laying in my money to painting up his house?"

She seized her shawl, threw it over her head, and rushed to the landlord's office.

"Oi weh! Mr. Landlord! Where is your heart? How could you raise me my rent when you know my son is yet in France? And even with the extra washing I take in I don't get enough when the eating is so dear?"

"The flat is worth five dollars more," answered Mr. Rosenblatt, impatiently. "I can get another tenant any minute."

"Have pity on me! I beg you! From where I can squeeze out the five dollars more for you?"

"That don't concern me. If you can't pay, somebody else will. I got to look out for myself. In America everybody looks out for himself."

"Is it nothing by you how I painted up your house with my own blood-money?"

"You didn't do it for me. You done it for yourself," he sneered. "It's nothing to me how the house looks, so long as I get my rent in time. You wanted to have a swell house, so you painted it. That's all."

With a wave of his hand he dismissed her.

"I beg by your conscience! Think on God!" Hanneh Hayyeh wrung her hands. "Ain't your house worth more to you to have a tenant clean it out and paint it out so beautiful like I done?"

"Certainly," snarled the landlord. "Because the flat is painted new, I can get more money for it. I got no more time for you."

He turned to his stenographer and resumed the dictation of his letters.

Dazedly Hanneh Hayyeh left the office. A choking dryness contracted her throat as she staggered blindly, gesticulating and talking to herself.

"Oi weh! The sweat, the money I laid into my flat and it should all go to the devil. And I should be turned out and leave all my beautifulness. And from where will I get the money for moving? When I begin to break myself up to move, I got to pay out money for the moving man, money for putting up new lines, money for new shelves and new hooks besides money for the rent. I got to remain where I am. But from where can I get together the five dollars for the robber? Should I go to Moisheh Itzek, the pawnbroker, or should I maybe ask Mrs. Preston? No—She shouldn't think I got her for a friend only to help me. Oi weh! Where should I turn with my bitter heart?"

Mechanically she halted at the butcher-shop. Throwing herself on the vacant bench, she buried her face in her shawl and burst out in a loud, heart-piercing wail: "Woe is me! Bitter is me!"

"Hanneh Hayyeh! What to you happened?" cried Mr. Sopkin in alarm.

His sympathy unlocked the bottom depths of her misery.

"Oi-i-i! Black is my luck! Dark is for my eyes!"

The butcher and the neighbors pressed close in upon her.

"Gewalt! What is it? Bad news from Aby in France?"

"Oi-i-i! The murderer! The thief! His gall should burst as mine is bursting! His heart should break as mine is breaking! It remains for me nothing but to be thrown out in the gutter. The landlord raised me five dollars a month rent. And he ripped yet my wounds by telling me he raised me the rent because my painted-up flat is so much more worth."

"The dogs! The blood-sucking landlords! They are the new czars from America!"

"What are you going to do?"

"What should I do? Aby is coming from France any day, and he's got to have a home to come to. I will have to take out from my eating the meat and the milk to save together the extra five dollars. People! Give me an advice! What else can I do? If a wild wolf falls on you in the black night, will crying help you?"

With a gesture of abject despair, she fell prone upon the bench. "Gottuniu! If there is any justice and mercy on this earth, then may the landlord be tortured like he is torturing me! May the fires burn him and the waters drown him! May his flesh be torn from him in pieces and his bones be ground in the teeth of wild dogs!"

Two months later, a wasted, haggard Hanneh Hayyeh stood in the kitchen, folding Mrs. Preston's wash in her basket, when the janitor—the servant of her oppressor—handed her another note.

"From the landlord," he said in his toneless voice.

Hanneh Hayyeh paled. She could tell from his smirking sneer that it was a second notice of increased rental.

It grew black before her eyes. She was too stunned to think. Her first instinct was to run to her husband; but she needed sympathy—not nagging. And then in her darkness she saw a light—the face of her friend, Mrs. Preston. She hurried to her.

"Oi—friend! The landlord raised me my rent again," she gasped, dashing into the room like a thing hounded by wild beasts.

Mrs. Preston was shocked by Hanneh Hayyeh's distraught appearance. For the first time she noticed the ravages of worry and hunger.

"Hanneh Hayyeh! Try to calm yourself. It is really quite inexcusable the way the landlords are taking advantage of the situation. There must be a way out. We'll fix it up somehow."

"How fix it up?" Hanneh Hayyeh flared.

"We'll see that you get the rent you need." There was reassurance and confidence in Mrs. Preston's tone.

Hanneh Hayyeh's eyes flamed. Too choked for utterance, her breath ceased for a moment.

"I want no charity! You think maybe I came to beg? No—I want justice!"

She shrank in upon herself, as though to ward off the raised whip of her persecutor. "You know how I feel?" Her voice came from the terrified depths of her. "It's as if the landlord pushed me in a corner and said to me: 'I want money, or I'll squeeze from you your life!' I have no money, so he takes my life.

"Last time, when he raised me my rent, I done without meat and without milk. What more can I do without?"

The piercing cry stirred Mrs. Preston as no mere words had done.

"Sometimes I get so weak for a piece of meat, I could tear the world to pieces. Hunger and bitterness are making a wild animal out of me. I ain't no more the same Hanneh Hayyeh I used to be."

The shudder that shook Hanneh Hayyeh communicated itself to Mrs. Preston. "I know the prices are hard to bear," she stammered, appalled.

"There used to be a time when poor people could eat cheap things," the toneless voice went on. "But now there ain't no more cheap things. Potatoes—rice—fish —even dry bread is dear. Look on my shoes! And I who used to be so neat with myself. I can't no more have my torn shoes fixed up. A pair of shoes or a little patch is only for millionaires."

"Something must be done," broke in Mrs. Preston, distraught for the first time in her life. "But in the meantime, Hanneh Hayyeh, you must accept this to tide you over." She spoke with finality as she handed her a bill.

Hanneh Hayyeh thrust back the money. "Ain't I hurt enough without you having to hurt me yet with charity? You want to give me hush money to swallow down an unrightness that burns my flesh? I want justice."

The woman's words were like bullets that shot through the static security of Mrs. Preston's life. She realized with a guilty pang that while strawberries and cream were being served at her table in January, Hanneh Hayyeh had doubtless gone without a square meal in months.

"We can't change the order of things overnight," faltered Mrs. Preston, baffled and bewildered by Hanneh Hayyeh's defiance of her proffered aid.

"Change things? There's got to be a change!" cried Hanneh Hayyeh with renewed intensity. "The world as it is is not to live in any longer. If only my Aby would get back quick. But until he comes, I'll fight till all America will have to stop and listen to me. You was always telling me that the lowest nobody got something to give to America. And that's what I got to give to America— the last breath in my body for justice. I'll wake up America from its sleep. I'll go myself to the President with my Aby's soldier picture and ask him was all this war to let loose a bunch of blood-suckers to suck the marrow out from the people?"

"Hanneh Hayyeh," said Mrs. Preston, with feeling, "these laws are far from just, but they are all we have so far. Give us time. We are young. We are still learning. We're doing our best."

Numb with suffering the woman of the ghetto looked straight into the eyes of Mrs. Preston. "And you too—you too hold by the landlord's side?—Oi—I see! Perhaps you too got property out by agents."

A sigh that had in it the resignation of utter hopelessness escaped from her. "Nothing can hurt me no more—And you always stood out to me in my dreams as the angel from love and beautifulness. You always made-believe to me that you're only for democracy."

Tears came to Mrs. Preston's eyes. But she made no move to defend herself or reply and Hanneh Hayyeh walked out in silence.

A few days later the whole block was astir with the news that Hanneh Hayyeh had gone to court to answer her dispossess summons.

From the windows, the stoop, from the hallway, and the doorway of the butcher-shop the neighbors were talking and gesticulating while waiting for Hanneh Hayyeh's return.

Hopeless and dead, Hanneh Hayyeh dragged herself to the butcher-shop. All made way for her to sit on the bench. She collapsed in a heap, not uttering a single sound, nor making a single move.

The butcher produced a bottle of brandy and, hastily filling a small glass, brought it to Hanneh Hayyeh.

"Quick, take it to your lips," he commanded. Weak from lack of food and exhausted by the ordeal of the court-room, Hanneh Hayyeh obeyed like a child.

Soon one neighbor came in with a cup of hot coffee; another brought bread and herring with onion over it.

Tense, breathless, with suppressed curiosity quivering on their lips, they waited till Hanneh Hayyeh swallowed the coffee and ate enough to regain a little strength.

"Nu? What became in the court?"

"What said the judge?"

"Did they let you talk yourself out like you said you would?"

"Was the murderer there to say something?"

Hanneh Hayyeh wagged her head and began talking

to herself in a low, toneless voice as if continuing her inward thought. "The judge said the same as Mrs. Preston said: the landlord has the right to raise our rent or put us out."

"Oi weh! If Hanneh Hayyeh with her fire in her mouth couldn't get her rights, then where are we?"

"To whom should we go? Who more will talk for us now?"

"Our life lays in their hands."

"They can choke us so much as they like!"

"Nobody cares. Nobody hears our cry!"

Out of this babel of voices there flashed across Hanneh Hayyeh's deadened senses the chimera that to her was the one reality of her aspiring soul—"Oi-i-i-i! My beautiful kitchen!" she sighed as in a dream.

The butcher's face grew red with wrath. His eyes gleamed like sharp, darting steel. "I wouldn't give that robber the satisfaction to leave your grand painted house," he said, turning to Hanneh Hayyeh. "I'd smash down everything for spite. You got nothing to lose. Such a murderer! I would learn him a lesson! 'An eye for an eye and a tooth for a tooth.'"

Hanneh Hayyeh, hair disheveled, clothes awry, the nails of her fingers dug in her scalp, stared with the glazed, impotent stare of a mad-woman. With unseeing eyes she rose and blindly made her way to her house.

As she entered her kitchen she encountered her husband hurrying in.

"Oi weh! Oi weh!" he whined. "I was always telling you your bad end. Everybody is already pointing their fingers on me! and all because you, a meshugeneh yideneh, a starved beggerin, talked it into your head that you got to have for yourself a white-painted kitchen alike to Mrs. Preston. Now you'll remember to listen to your husband. Now, when you'll be laying in the street to shame and to laughter for the whole world."

"Out! Out from my sight! Out from my house!" shrieked Hanneh Hayyeh. In her rage she seized a flat-iron and Jake heard her hurl it at the slammed door as he fled downstairs.

It was the last night before the eviction. Hanneh Hayyeh gazed about her kitchen with tear-glazed eyes. "Some one who got nothing but only money will come in here and get the pleasure from all this beautifulness that cost me the blood from my heart. Is this already America? What for was my Aby fighting? Was it then only a dream—all these millions people from all lands and from all times, wishing and hoping and praying that America is? Did I wake myself from my dreaming to see myself back in the black times of Russia under the czar?"

Her eager, beauty-loving face became distorted with hate. "No—the landlord ain't going to get the best from me! I'll learn him a lesson. 'An eye for an eye'—"

With savage fury, she seized the chopping-axe and began to scratch down the paint, breaking the plaster on the walls. She tore up the floor-boards. She unscrewed the gas-jets, turned on the gas full force so as to blacken the white-painted ceiling. The night through she raged with the frenzy of destruction.

Utterly spent she flung herself on the lounge, but she could not close her eyes. Her nerves quivered. Her body ached, and she felt her soul ache there—inside her—like a thing killed that could not die.

The first grayness of dawn filtered through the air-shaft window of the kitchen. The room was faintly lighted, and as the rays of dawn got stronger and reached farther, one by one the things she had mutilated in the night started, as it were, into consciousness. She looked at her dish-closet, once precious, that she had scratched and defaced; the uprooted geranium-box on the window-sill; the marred walls. It was unbearable all this waste and desolation that stared at her. "Can it be I who done all this?" she asked herself. "What devil got boiling in me?"

What had she gained by her rage for vengeance? She had thought to spite the landlord, but it was her own soul she had killed. These walls that stared at her in their ruin were not just walls. They were animate—they throbbed with the pulse of her own flesh. For every inch of the broken plaster there was a scar on her heart. She had destroyed that which had taken her so many years of prayer and longing to build up. But this de-molished beauty like her own soul, though killed, still quivered and ached with the unstilled pain of life. "Oi weh!" she moaned, swaying to and fro. "So much lost beautifulness—"

Private Abraham Safransky, with the look in his eyes and the swing of his shoulders of all the boys who come back from overseas, edged his way through the wet Delancey Street crowds with the skill of one born to these streets and the assurance of the United States Army. Fresh from the ship, with a twenty-four-hour leave stowed safely in his pocket, he hastened to see his people after nearly two years' separation.

On Private Safransky's left shoulder was the insignia of the Statue of Liberty. The three gold service stripes on his left arm and the two wound stripes of his right were supplemented by the Distinguished Service Medal on his left breast bestowed by the United States Government.

As he pictured his mother's joy when he would surprise her in her spotless kitchen, the soldier broke into the double-quick.

All at once he stopped; on the sidewalk before their house was a heap of household things that seemed familiar and there on the curbstone a woman huddled, cowering, broken.—Good God—his mother! His own mother—and all their worldly belongings dumped there in the rain.

The Lord Giveth

One glance at his wife's tight-drawn mouth warned Reb
Ravinsky of the torrent of wrath about to burst over
his head.

"*Nu,* my bread-giver? Did you bring me the rent?"
she hurled at him between clenched teeth.

Reb Ravinsky had promised to borrow money that
morning to ward off their impending eviction for unpaid
rent, but no sooner had he stepped out of his house than
all thought of it fled from his mind. Instinctively, he
turned to the synagog where he had remained all day
absorbed in the sacred script. It was easier to pray and
soar the heights with the prophets of his race than to
wrestle with sordid, earthly cares.

"Holy Jew! Why didn't you stay away a little longer?"
She tore at her wig in her fury. "Are you a man like other
men? Does your wife or your child lay in your head at
all? I got to worry for rent. I got to worry for bread. If
you got to eat you eat. If you ain't got to eat you ain't
hungry. You fill yourself only with high thoughts. You
hold yourself only with God. Your wife and your child
can be thrown in the street to shame and to laughter.
But what do you care? You live only for the next world.
You got heaven in your head. The rest of your family
can rot in hell."

Reb Ravinsky stood mute and helpless under the
lash of her tongue. But when she had exhausted her
store of abuse, he cast upon her a look of scorn and
condemnation.

"*Ishah Rah! Evil woman!*" he turned upon her like an
ancient prophet denouncing ungodliness.

125

"*Ishah Rah!*" he repeated. His voice of icy passion sent shivers up and down her spine.

"*Ishah Rah!*" came for the third time with the mystic solemnity that subdued her instantly into worshipful subjection. "Tear away your man from God! Tear him away from the holy Torah! Lose the one precious thing in life, the one thing that makes a Jew stand out over all other nations of the world, the one thing that the Czar's *pogroms* and all the sufferings and murders of the Jews could not kill in the Jew—the hope for the next world!"

Like a towering spirit of righteousness afire with the word of God he loomed over her.

"I ask you by your conscience, should I give up the real life, the true life, for good eating, good sleeping, for a life in the body like the *Amoratzim* here in America? Should I make from the Torah a pick with which to dig for you the rent?"

Adjusting his velvet skull-cap, the last relic of his rabbinical days, he caught the woman's adoring look. Memories of his past splendor in Russia surged over him. He saw his people coming to him from far and near to learn wisdom from his lips. Drawing himself to his full height, he strode across the room and faced her.

"Why didn't you marry yourself to a tailor, a shoe-maker, a thick-head, a money-maker—to a man of the flesh—a rabbi who can sell his religion over the counter as a butcher sells meat?"

Mrs. Ravinsky gazed with fear and contrition at her husband's God-kindled face. She loved him because he was *not* a man of this world. Her darkest moments were lit up with pride in him, with the hope that in the next world the reflected glory of his piety might exalt her.

It wrung her heart to realize that against her will she was dragging him down with her ceaseless demands for bread and rent. *Ach!* Why was there such an evil thing as money in this world? Why did she have to torture her husband with earthly needs when all she longed for was to help him win a higher place in heaven?

Tears fell from her faded eyes. He could have wept with her—it hurt him so to make her suffer. But once and for all he must put a stop to her nagging. He must cast out the evil spirit of worry that possessed her lest it turn and rend him.

"Why are you killing yourself so for this life? *Ut!* See, death is already standing over you. One foot is already in the grave. Do you know what you'll get for making nothing from the Torah! The fires of hell are waiting for you! Wait—wait! I warn you!"

And as if to ward off the devil that threatened his house, he rushed to his shrine of sacred books and pulled from its niche a volume of his beloved Talmud. With reverence he caressed its worn and yellowed pages as he drank in hungrily the inspired words. For a few blessed moments he took refuge from all earthly storms.

II

In Schnipishock, Reb Ravinsky had been a Porush, a pensioned scholar. The Jews of the village so deeply appreciated his learning and piety that they granted him an allowance, so as to free the man of God from all earthly cares.

Arrived in the new world, he soon learned that there was no honored pension forthcoming to free him from the world of the flesh. For a time he eked out a bare living by teaching Hebrew to private scholars. But the opening of the Free Hebrew Schools resulted in the loss of most of his pupils.

He had been chosen by God to spread the light of the

Torah—and a living must come to him, somehow, somewhere, if he only served faithfully.

In the meantime, how glorious it was to suffer hunger and want, even shame and derision, yet rise through it all as Job had risen and proclaim to the world: "I know that my Redeemer liveth!"

Reb Ravinsky was roused from his ecstacy by his wife's loud sobbing. Thrust out from the haven of his Torah, he closed the book and began to pace the floor.

"Can fire and water go together? Neither can godliness and an easy life. If you have eyes of flesh and are blind, should I fall into your blindness? You care only for what you can put in your mouth or wear on your back; I struggle for the life that is together with God!"

"My rent—have you my rent? I warned you!" The landlord pushed through the half-open door flaunting his final dispossess notice under Reb Ravinsky's nose. "I got orders to put you out," he gloated, as he motioned to his men to proceed with the eviction.

Reb Ravinsky gripped the back of a chair for support.

"*Oi-i-i!* Black is me! Bitter is me!" groaned his wife, leaning limply against the wall.

For weeks she had been living in momentary dread of this catastrophe. Now, when the burly moving-men actually broke into her home, she surrendered herself to the anguish of utter defeat. She watched them disconnect the rusty stove and carry it into the street. They took the bed, the Passover dishes prayerfully wrapped to avoid the soil of leavened bread. They took the brass samovar and the Sabbath candlesticks. And she stood mutely by—defenseless—impotent!

"What did I sin?" The cry broke from her. "God! God! Is there a God over us and sees all this?"

The men and the things they touched were to Reb

Ravinsky's far-seeing eyes as shadows of the substance-less dream of life in the flesh. With vision focussed on the next world, he saw in dim blurs the drama enacted in this world.

Smash to the floor went the sacred Sabbath wine-glass! Reb Ravinsky turned sharply, in time to see a man tumble ruthlessly the sacred Hebrew books to the floor.

A flame of holy wrath leaped from the old man's eyes. His breath came in convulsive gasps as he clutched with emaciated fingers at his heart. The sacrilege of the ruffians! He rushed to pick up the books, kissing each volume with pious reverence. As he gathered them in his trembling arms, he looked about confusedly for a safe hiding-place. In his anxiety for the safety of his holy treasure, he forgot the existence of his wife and ran with his books to the synagog as one runs from a house on fire. So overwrought was he that he nearly fell over his little daughter running up the stairs.

"Murderer!" screamed Mrs. Ravinsky, after him. "Run, run to the synagog! Holy Jew! See where your religion has brought us. Run—ask God to pay your rent!"

She turned to her little Rachel who burst into the room terrified.

"See, my heart! See what they've done to us! And your father ran to hide himself in the synagog. You got no father—nobody to give you bread. A lost orphan you are."

"Will the charity lady have to bring us eating again?" asked Rachel, her eyes dilated with dread. "Wait only till I get old enough to go to the shop and earn money." And she reached up little helpless arms protectingly.

The child's sympathy was as salt on the mother's wounds.

"For what did we come to America?"

The four walls of her broken home stared back their answer.

Only the bundles of bedding remained, which Rachel guarded with fierce defiance as tho she would save it from the wreckage.

Pushing the child roughly aside, the man slung it over his shoulder. Mrs. Ravinsky, with Rachel holding on to her skirts, felt her way after him, down the dark stairway.

"My life! My blood! My featherbed! .. she cried, as he tossed the family heirloom into the gutter. "*Gevalt!*" prostrate, she fell on it. "How many winters it took my mother to pick together the feathers! My mother's wedding present...."

III

From the stoops, the alleys, and the doorways, the neighbors gathered. Hanneh Breineh, followed by her clinging brood, pushed through the throng, her red-lidded eyes big with compassion. "Come the while in by me."

She helped the grief-stricken woman to her feet. "We're packed like herring in a barrel, but there's always room for a push-in of a few more."

Lifting the feather-bed under her arm she led the way to her house.

"In a few more years your Rachel will be old enough to get her working-papers and all your worries for bread will be over," she encouraged, as she opened the door of her stuffy little rooms.

The commotion on the street corner broke in upon the babble of gossiping women in the butcher shop. Mr. Sopkin paused in cutting the meat.

"Who did they make to move?" he asked, joining the gesticulating mob at the doorway.

"*Oi weh!* Reb Ravinsky?"

"God from the sky! Such a good Jew! Such a light for the world!"

"Home, in Russia, they kissed the ground on which he walked, and in America, they throw him in the street."

"Who cares in America for religion? In America, everybody has his head in his belly."

"Poor little Rachel! Such a smart child! Writes letters for everybody on the block."

"Such a lazy do-nothing! All day in the synagog!" flung the pawnbroker's wife, a big-bosomed woman, her thick fingers covered with diamonds. "Why don't he go to work in a shop?"

A neighbor turned upon her. "Here! Hear her only! Such a pig-eater! Such a fat-head! She dares take Reb Ravinsky's name in her mouth."

"Who was she from home? A water-carrier's wife, a cook! And in America she makes herself for a person— shines up the street with her diamonds."

"Then leave somebody let know the charities." With a gesture of self-defense, the pawnbroker's wife fingered her gold beads. "I'm a lady-member from the charities."

"The charities? A black year on them!" Came a chorus of angry voices.

"All my enemies should have to go to the charities for help."

"Woe to anyone who falls into the charities' hands!"

"One poor man with a heart can help more than the charities with all their money."

Mr. Sopkin hammered on his chopping-block, his face purple with excitement. "*Weiber!* with talk alone you can't fill up the pot."

"*Takeh! Takeh!*" Eager faces strained forward. "Let's put outselves together for a collection."

"I'm not yet making Rockefeller's millions from the

butcher business, but still, here's my beginning for good luck." And Mr. Sopkin tossed a dollar bill into the basket on the counter.

A woman, a ragged shawl over her head, clutched a quarter in her gaunt hand. "God is my witness! To tear out this from my pocket is like tearing off my right hand. I need every cent to keep the breath in the bodies of my *Kinder,* but how can we let such a holy Jew fall in the street?"

"My enemies should have to slave with such bitter sweat for every penny as me." Hanneh Hayyeh flung out her arms still wet with soapsuds and kissed the ten-cent piece she dropped into the collection.

Mr. Sopkin walked to the sidewalk and shook the basket in front of the passers-by. "Take your hand out from your pocket! Take your bite away from your mouth! Who will help the poor if not the poor?"

A shower of coins came pouring in. It seemed not money—but the flesh and blood of the people—each coin a part of a living heart.

The pawnbroker's wife, shamed by the surging generosity of the crowd, grudgingly peeled a dollar from the roll of bills in her stocking and started to put it into the collection.

A dozen hands lifted in protest.

"No—no! Your money and our money can't mix together!"

"Our money is us—our bodies! Yours is the profits from the pawnshop! Hold your *trefah* dollar for the charities!"

IV

Only when the Shammes, the caretaker of the synagog, rattling his keys, shook Reb Ravinsky gently and reminded him that it was past closing time did he remember that somewhere waiting for him—perhaps in the street—were his wife and child.

The happening of the day had only deepened the intensity with which he clung to God and His Torah. His lips still moved in habitual prayer as with the guidance of neighbors he sought the new flat which had been rented for a month with the collection money.

Bread, butter, milk, and eggs greeted his gaze as he opened the door.

"*Nu*, my wife? Is there a God over us?" His face kindled with guileless faith. "The God that feeds the little fishes in the sea and the birds in the air, has he not fed us? You see, the Highest One takes care of our earthly needs. Our only business here is to pray for holiness to see His light!"

A cloud of gloom stared up at him out of his wife's darkening eyes. "Why are you still so black with worry?" he admonished. "If you would only trust yourself on God, all good would come to us yet."

"On my enemies should fall the good that has come to us," groaned Mrs. Ravinsky. "Better already death than to be helped again by the pity from kind people."

"What difference how the help comes, so long we can keep up our souls to praise God for His mercy on us?"

Despair was in the look she fixed upon her husband's lofty brow—a brow untouched by time or care—smooth, calm, and seamless as a child's. "No wonder people think that I'm your mother. The years make you younger. You got no blood in your body—no feelings in your heart. I got to close my eyes with shame to pass in the street the people who helped me, while you—you—shame cannot shame you—poverty can not crush you—"

"Poverty? It stands in the Talmud that poverty is an

ornament on a Jew like a red ribbon on a white horse. Those whom God chooses for His next world can't have it good here."

"Stop feeding me with the next world!" she flung at him in her exasperation. "Give me something on this world."

"Wait only till our American daughter will grow up. That child has my head on her," he boasted with a father's pride. "Wait only, you'll see the world will ring from her yet. With the Hebrew learning I gave her, she'll shine out from all other American children."

"But how will she be able to lift her head with other people alike if you depend yourself on the charities?"

"Woman! Worry yourself not for our Rachel! It stands in the Holy Book, the world is a wheel, always turning. Those who are rich get poor; if not they, then their children or children's children. And those who are poor like us, go up higher and higher. Our daughter will yet be so rich, she'll give away money to the charities that helped us. Isaiah said—"

"Enough—enough!" broke in Mrs. Ravinsky, thrilled in spite of herself by the prophecies of her holy man. "I know already all your smartness. Go, go, sit yourself down and eat something. You fasted all day."

V

Mrs. Ravinsky hoarded for her husband and child the groceries the neighbors had donated. For herself, she allowed only the left-overs, the crums, and crusts.

The following noon, after finishing her meager meal, she still felt the habitual gnawing of her undernourished body, so she took a sour pickle and cut off another slice of bread from the dwindling loaf. But this morsel only sharpened her craving for more food.

The lingering savor of the butter and eggs which she

had saved for her family tantalized her starved nerves. Faint and weak from the struggle to repress her hunger, she grew reckless and for once in her life abandoned herself to the gluttonous indulgence of the best in her scant larder.

With shaking hand, she stealthily opened the cupboard, pilfered a knife-load of butter and spread it thickly on a second slice of bread. Cramming the whole into her mouth, she snatched two eggs and broke them into the frying pan. The smell of the sizzling eggs filled the air with the sweet fragrance of the Sabbath. "*Ach!* How the sun would shine in my heart if I could only allow myself the bite in my mouth!"

Memories of *gefullte fisch* and the odor of freshly-baked *apfel strudel* dilated her nostrils. She saw herself back in Russia setting the Sabbath table when she was the honored wife of Reb Ravinsky.

The sudden holiday feeling that thrilled her senses smote her conscience. "*Oi weh!* Sinner that I am! Why should it will itself in me to eat like a person when my man don't earn enough for dry bread? What will we do when this is used up? Suppose the charities should catch me feasting myself with such a full hand?"

Bent ravenously over the eggs—one eye on the door—she lifted the first spoonful to her watering mouth as Rachel flew in, eyes wide with excitement.

"Mamma! The charity lady is coming! She's asking the fish-peddler on the stoop where we live now."

"Quick! Hide the frying-pan in the oven. Woe is me! The house not swept—dishes not washed—everything thrown around! Rachel! Quick only—sweep together the dirt in a corner. Throw those rags under the bed! *Oi weh*—quick—hide all those dirty things behind the trunk!"

In her haste to tidy up, she remembered the food in

the cupboard. She stuffed it—broken eggshells and all—into the bureau drawer. "*Oi weh!* The charity lady should only not catch us with all these holiday eatings...."

VI

Footsteps in the hallway and Miss Naughton's cheery voice: "Here I am, Mrs. Ravinsky! What can I do to help now?"

With the trained eye of the investigator, she took in the wretched furniture, scant bedding, the undernourished mother and child.

"What seems to be wrong?" Miss Naughton drew up a three-legged stool. "Won't you tell me so we can get at the root of the trouble? She put her hand on the woman's apron with a friendly little gesture.

Mrs. Ravinsky bit her lips to force back the choking pressure of tears. The life, the buoyancy, the very kindness of the "charity lady" stabbed deeper the barb of her wretchedness.

"Woe is me! On all my enemies my black heart! So many babies and young people die every day, but no death comes to hide me from my shame."

"Don't give way like that," pleaded Miss Naughton, pained by the bitterness that she tried in vain to understand. "If you will only tell me a few things so I may the better know how to help you."

"Again tear me in pieces with questions?" Mrs. Ravinsky pulled at the shrunken skin of her neck.

"I don't like to pry into your personal affairs, but if you only knew how often we're imposed upon. Last week we had a case of a woman who asked us to pay her rent. When I called to investigate, I found her cooking chicken for dinner!"

The cot on which Mrs. Ravinsky sat creaked under her swaying body.

"You see, we have only a small amount of money," went on the unconscious inquisitor, "and it is but fair it should go to the most deserving cases."

Entering a few preliminary notes, Miss Naughton looked up inquiringly. "Where is Mr. Ravinsky?"

"In the synagog."

"Has he no work?"

"He can't do no work. His head is on the next world."

Miss Naughton frowned. She was accustomed to this kind of excuse. "People who are not lazy can always find employment."

Seeing Mrs. Ravinsky's sudden pallor, she added kindly: "You have not eaten to-day. Is there no food in the house?"

Mrs. Ravinsky staggered blindly to her feet. "No—nothing—I didn't yet eat nothing."

The brooding gray of Rachel's eyes darkened with shame as she clutched protectingly at her mother's apron. The uncanny, old look of the solemn little face seemed to brush against Miss Naughton's very heart-strings—to reproach the rich vigor of her own glowing youth.

"Have you had any lunch, dear?" The "charity lady's" hand rested softly on the tangled mat of hair.

"N-nothing—nothing," the child echoed her mother's words.

Miss Naughton rose abruptly. She dared not let her feelings get the best of her. "I am going to get some groceries." She sought for an excuse to get away for a moment from the misery that overwhelmed her. "I'll be back soon."

"Bitter is me!" wailed Mrs. Ravinsky, as the "charity

lady" left the room. "I can never lift up my head with
other people alike. I feel myself lower than a thief, just
because I got a husband who holds himself with God
all day."

She cracked the knuckles of her bony fingers. "*Gottuniu!* Listen better to my prayer! Send on him only a
quick death. Maybe if I was a widow, people would take
pity on me and save me from this gehenna of charity."

VII

Ten minutes later, Miss Naughton returned with a
bag of supplies. "I am going to fix some lunch for you."
She measured cocoa into a battered saucepan. "And
soon the boy will come with enough groceries for the
whole week."

"Please, please," begged Mrs. Ravinsky. "I can't eat
now—I can't—."

"But the child? She needs nutritious food at once."

Rachel's sunken little chest rose and fell with her
frightened heartbeat, as she hid her face in her mother's
lap.

"Small as she is, she already feels how it hurts to
swallow charity eating," defended Mrs. Ravinsky.

Miss Naughton could understand the woman's dis-
like of accepting charity. She had coped with this pride of
the poor before. But she had no sympathy with this
mother who fostered resentment in her child toward
the help that was so urgently needed. Miss Naughton's
long-suffering patience broke. She turned from the stove
and resolutely continued her questioning.

"Has your husband tried our employment bureau?"

"No."

"Then send him to our office to-morrow at nine. He
can be a janitor—or a porter—"

"My man? My man a janitor or a porter?" Her eyes
flamed. "Do you know who was my man in Russia? The
fat of the land they brought him just for the pleasure to
listen to his learning. Barrels full of meat, pots full of
chicken-fat stood packed in my cellar. I used to make
boilers of jelly at a time. The *gefüllte fisch* only I gave away
is more than the charities give out to the poor in
a month."

Miss Naughton could not suppress a smile. "Why did
you leave it then, if it was all so perfect?"

"My *gefüllte fisch*! Oi-i-i! Oi-i! My *apfel strudel*—my
beautiful *apfel strudel*!" she kept repeating, unable to
tear herself away from the dream of the past.

Can you live on the *apfel strudel* you had in Russia?
In America, a man must work to support his family—"

"All thick-heads support their families," defended
Reb Ravinsky's wife. "Any fat-belly can make money.
My man is a light for the world. He works for God who
feeds even the worms under the stone."

"You send your husband to my office. I want to have
a talk with him."

"To your office? *Gottuniu!* He won't go. In Schnipishock they came to him from the four ends of the world.
The whole town blessed itself with his religiousness."

"The first principle of religion is for a man to provide
for his family. You must do exactly as we say—or we
cannot help you."

"Please, please." Mrs. Ravinsky entreated, cringing
and begging. "We got no help from nobody now but you.
I'll bring him to your office to-morrow."

The investigator now proceeded with the irksome
duty of her more formal questions. "How much rent do
you pay? Do you keep any boarders? Does your husband
belong to any society or lodge? Have you relatives who
are able to help you?"

"*Oi-i-i!* What more do you want from me?" shrieked the distracted woman.

Having completed her questions, Miss Naughton looked about the room. "I am sorry to speak of it, but why is your flat in such disorder?"

"I only moved in yesterday. I didn't get yet time to fix it up."

"But it was just as bad in the last place. If you want our help you must do your part. Soap and water are cheap. Anyone can be clean."

The woman's knees gave way under her, as Miss Naughton lifted the lids from the pots on the stove.

And then—*gevalt!* It grew black before Mrs. Ravinsky's eyes. She collapsed into a pathetic heap to the floor. The "charity lady" opened the oven door and exposed the tell-tale frying pan and the two eggs!

Eyes of silent condemnation scorched through the terror-stricken creature whose teeth chattered in a vain struggle to defend herself. But no voice came from her tortured throat. She could only clutch at her child in a panic of helplessness.

Without a word, the investigator began to search through every nook and corner and at last she came to the bureau drawer and found butter, eggs, cheese, bread, and even a jar of jelly.

"For shame!" broke from the wounded heart of the betrayed Miss Naughton. "You—you ask for charity!"

VIII

In the hall below, Reb Ravinsky, returning from the synagog, encountered a delivery boy.

"Where live the Ravinskys?" the lad questioned.

"I'm Reb Ravinsky," he said, leading the way, as he saw the boxes of groceries.

Followed by the boy, Reb Ravinsky flung open the door and strode joyfully into the room. "Look only! How the manna is falling from the sky!"

Ignoring Reb Ravinsky, Miss Naughton motioned to the box. "Take those things right back," she commanded the boy.

"How you took me in with your hungry look!" There was more of sorrow than scorn in her voice. "Even teaching your child to lie—and your husband a rabbi!—a religious man—too holy to work! What would be left for deserving cases, if we allowed such as you to defraud legitimate charity?"

With bowed head, Reb Ravinsky closed the door after the departing visitor. The upbraidings of the woman were like a whip-lash on his naked flesh. His heart ached for his helpless family. Darkness suffocated him.

"My hungry little lamb," wailed his wife, clinging to Rachel. "Where now can we turn for bread?"

Compassionate hands reached out in prayer over the grief-stricken mother and child. Reb Ravinsky stood again as he did before his flight to America, facing his sorrowing people. His wife's wailing for their lost store of bread brought back to him the bereaved survivors of the *pogrom*—the *pogrom* that snatched away their sons and daughters. Afire with the faith of his race, he chanted the age-old consolation. "The Lord giveth; the Lord taketh away. Blessed be the name of the Lord."

III

SUCCESS

Children of Loneliness

Oh, Mother, can't you use a fork?" exclaimed Rachel as Mrs. Ravinsky took the shell of the baked potato in her fingers and raised it to her watering mouth.

"Here, *Teacherin* mine, you want to learn me in my old age how to put the bite in my mouth?" The mother dropped the potato back into her plate, too wounded to eat. Wiping her hands on her blue-checked apron, she turned her glance to her husband, at the opposite side of the table.

"Yankev," she said bitterly, "stick your bone on a fork. Our *teacherin* said you dassn't touch no eatings with the hands."

"All my teachers died already in the old country," retorted the old man. "I ain't going to learn nothing new no more from my American daughter." He continued to suck the marrow out of the bone with that noisy relish that was so exasperating to Rachel.

"It's no use," stormed the girl, jumping up from the table in disgust; "I'll never be able to stand it here with you people."

"'You people?' What do you mean by 'you people?'" shouted the old man, lashed into fury by his daughter's words. "You think you got a different skin from us because you went to college?"

"It drives me wild to hear you crunching bones like savages. If you people won't change, I shall have to move and live by myself."

Yankev Ravinsky threw the half-gnawed bone upon the table with such vehemence that a plate broke into fragments.

"You witch you!" he cried in a hoarse voice tense with rage. "Move by yourself! We lived without you while you was away in college, and we can get on without you further. God ain't going to turn his nose on us because we ain't got table manners from America. A hell she made from this house since she got home."

"*Shah!* Yankev *leben*," pleaded the mother, "the neighbors are opening the windows to listen to our hollering. Let us have a little quiet for a while till the eating is over."

But the accumulated hurts and insults that the old man had borne in the one week since his daughter's return from college had reached the breaking-point. His face was convulsed, his eyes flashed, and his lips were flecked with froth as he burst out in a volley of scorn:

"You think you can put our necks in a chain and learn us new tricks? You think you can make us over for Americans? We got through till fifty years of our lives eating in our own old way—"

"Woe is me, Yankev *leben!*" entreated his wife. "Why can't we choke ourselves with our troubles? Why must the whole world know how we are tearing ourselves by the heads? In all Essex Street, in all New York, there ain't such fights like by us."

Her pleadings were in vain. There was no stopping Yankev Ravinsky once his wrath was roused. His daughter's insistence upon the use of a knife and fork spelled apostasy, anti-Semitism, and the aping of the Gentiles.

Like a prophet of old condemning unrighteousness, he ran the gamut of denunciation, rising to heights of fury that were sublime and godlike, and sinking from sheer exhaustion to abusive bitterness.

"*Pfui* on all your American colleges! *Pfui* on the morals of America! No respect for old age. No feat for God.

Stepping with your feet on all the laws of the holy Torah. A fire should burn out the whole new generation. They should sink into the earth, like Korah."

"Look at him cursing and burning! Just because I insist on their changing their terrible table manners. One would think I was killing them."

"Do you got to use a gun to kill?" cried the old man, little red threads darting out of the whites of his eyes.

"Who is doing the killing? Aren't you choking the life out of me? Aren't you dragging me by the hair to the darkness of past ages every minute of the day? I'd die of shame if one of my college friends should open the door while you people are eating."

"You—you—"

The old man was on the point of striking his daughter when his wife seized the hand he raised.

"Mincha! Yankev, you forgot *Mincha!"*

This reminder was a flash of inspiration on Mrs. Ravinsky's part, the only thing that could have ended the quarreling instantly. *Mincha* was the prayer just before sunset of the orthodox Jews. This religious rite was so automatic with the old man that at his wife's mention of *Mincha* everything was immediately shut out, and Yankev Ravinsky rushed off to a corner of the room to pray.

"Ashrai Yoishwai Waisahuh!"

"Happy are they who dwell in Thy house. Ever shall I praise Thee. *Selah!* Great is the Lord, and exceedingly to be praised; and His greatness is unsearchable. On the majesty and glory of Thy splendor, and on Thy marvelous deeds, will I meditate."

The shelter from the storms of life that the artist finds in his art, Yankev Ravinsky found in his prescribed communion with God. All the despair caused by his daughter's apostasy, the insults and disappointments he suffered, were in his sobbing voice. But as he entered into the spirit of his prayer, he felt the man of flesh drop away in the outflow of God around him. His voice mellowed, the rigid wrinkles of his face softened, the hard glitter of anger and condemnation in his eyes was transmuted into the light of love as he went on:

"The Lord is gracious and merciful; slow to anger and of great loving-kindness. To all that call upon Him in truth He will hear their cry and save them."

Oblivious to the passing and repassing of his wife as she warmed anew the unfinished dinner, he continued:

"Put not your trust in princes, in the son of man in whom there is no help." Here Reb Ravinsky paused long enough to make a silent confession for the sin of having placed his hope on his daughter instead of on God. His whole body bowed with the sense of guilt. Then in a moment his humility was transfigured into exaltation. Sorrow for sin dissolved in joy as he became more deeply aware of God's unfailing protection.

"Happy is he who hath the God of Jacob for his help, whose hope is in the Lord his God. He healeth the broken in heart, and bindeth up their wounds."

A healing balm filled his soul as he returned to the table, where the steaming hot food awaited him. Rachel sat near the window pretending to read a book. Her mother did not urge her to join them at the table, fearing another outbreak, and the meal continued in silence.

The girl's thoughts surged hotly as she glanced from her father to her mother. A chasm of four centuries could not have separated her more completely from them than her four years at Cornell.

"To think that I was born of these creatures! It's an insult to my soul. What kinship have I with these two lumps of ignorance and superstition? They're ugly and gross and stupid. I'm all sensitive nerves. They want to wallow in dirt."

She closed her eyes to shut out the sight of her parents as they silently ate together, unmindful of the dirt and confusion.

"How is it possible that I lived with them and like them only four years ago? What is it in me that so quickly gets accustomed to the best? Beauty and cleanliness are as natural to me as if I'd been born on Fifth Avenue instead of the dirt of Essex Street."

A vision of Frank Baker passed before her. Her last long talk with him out under the trees in college still lingered in her heart. She felt that she had only to be with him again to carry forward the beautiful friendship that had sprung up between them. He had promised to come shortly to New York. How could she possibly introduce such a born and bred American to her low, ignorant, dirty parents?

"I might as well tear the thought of Frank Baker out of my heart," she told herself. "If he just once sees the pigsty of a home I come from, if he just sees the table manners of my father and mother, he'll fly through the ceiling."

Timidly, Mrs. Ravinsky turned to her daughter.

"Ain't you going to give a taste the eating?"

No answer.

"I fried the *lotkes* special' for you—"

"I can't stand your fried, greasy stuff."

"Ain't even my cooking good no more either?" Her gnarled, hard-worked hands clutched at her breast. "God from the world, for what do I need yet any more my life? Nothing I do for my child is no use no more."

Her head sank; her whole body seemed to shrivel and grow old with the sense of her own futility.

"How I was hurrying to run by the butcher before everybody else, so as to pick out the grandest, fattest piece of *brust!*" she wailed, tears streaming down her face. "And I put my hand away from my heart and put a whole fresh egg into the *lotkes,* and I stuffed the stove full of coal like a millionaire so as to get the *lotkes* fried so nice and brown; and now you give a kick on everything I done—

"Fool woman," shouted her husband, "stop laying yourself on the ground for your daughter to step on you! What more can you expect from a child raised up in America? What more can you expect but that she should spit in your face and make dirt from you?" His eyes, hot and dry under their lids, flashed from his wife to his daughter. "The old Jewish eating is poison to her; she must have *trefa* ham—only forbidden food."

Bitter laughter shook him.

"Woman, how you patted yourself with pride before all the neighbors, boasting of our great American daughter coming home from college! This is our daughter, our pride, our hope, our pillow for our old age that we were dreaming about! This is our American *teacherin!* A Jew-hater, an anti-Semite we brought into the world, a betrayer of our race who hates her own father and mother like the Russian Czar once hated a Jew. She makes herself so refined, she can't stand it when we use the knife or fork the wrong way; but her heart is that of a brutal Cossack, and she spills her own father's and mother's blood like water."

Every word he uttered seared Rachel's soul like burning acid. She felt herself becoming a witch, a she-devil, under the spell of his accusations.

"You want me to love you yet?" She turned upon her father like an avenging fury. "If there's any evil hatred in my soul, you have roused it with your cursed preaching."

"*Oi-i-i!* Highest One! pity Yourself on us!" Mrs. Ravinsky wrung her hands. "Rachel, Yankev, let there be an end to this knife-stabbing! *Gottuniu!* my flesh is torn to pieces!"

Unheeding her mother's pleading, Rachel rushed to the closet where she kept her things.

"I was a crazy idiot to think that I could live with you people under one roof." She flung on her hat and coat and bolted for the door.

Mrs. Ravinsky seized Rachel's arm in passionate entreaty.

"My child, my heart, my life, what do you mean? Where are you going?

"I mean to get out of this hell of a home this very minute," she said, tearing loose from her mother's clutching hands.

"Woe is me! My child! We'll be to shame and to laughter by the whole world. What will people say?"

"Let them say! My life is my own; I'll live as I please." She slammed the door in her mother's face.

"They want me to love them yet," ran the mad thoughts in Rachel's brain as she hurried through the streets, not knowing where she was going, not caring. "Vampires, bloodsuckers fastened on my flesh! Black shadow blighting every ray of light that ever came my way! Other parents scheme and plan and wear themselves out to give their child a chance, but they put dead stones in front of every chance I made for myself."

With the cruelty of youth to everything not youth, Rachel reasoned:

"They have no rights, no claims over me like other parents who do things for their children. It was my own brains, my own courage, my own iron will that forced my way out of the sweatshop to my present position in the public schools. I owe them nothing, nothing, nothing."

II

Two weeks already away from home. Rachel looked about her room. It was spotlessly clean. She had often said to herself while at home with her parents: "All I want is an empty room, with a bed, a table, and a chair. As long as it is clean and away from them, I'll be happy." But was she happy?

A distant door closed, followed by the retreating sound of descending footsteps. Then all was still, the stifling stillness of a rooming-house. The white, empty walls pressed in upon her, suffocated her. She listened acutely for any stir of life, but the continued silence was unbroken save for the insistent ticking of her watch.

"I ran away from home burning for life," she mused, "and all I've found is the loneliness that's death." A wave of self-pity weakened her almost to the point of tears. "I'm alone! I'm alone!" she moaned, crumpling into a heap.

"Must it always be with me like this," her soul cried in terror, "either to live among those who drag me down or in the awful isolation of a hall bedroom? Oh, I'll die of loneliness among these frozen, each-shut-in-himself Americans! It's one thing to break away, but, oh, the strength to go on alone! How can I ever do it? The love instinct is so strong in me; I can not live without love, without people."

The thought of a letter from Frank Baker suddenly lightened her spirits. That very evening she was to meet him for dinner. Here was hope—more than hope. Just seeing him again would surely bring the certainty.

This new rush of light upon her dark horizon so softened her heart that she could almost tolerate her superfluous parents.

"If I could only have love and my own life, I could almost forgive them for bringing me into the world. I don't really hate them; I only hate them when they stand between me and the new America that I'm to conquer."

Answering her impulse, her feet led her to the familiar Ghetto streets. On the corner of the block where her parents lived she paused, torn between the desire to see her people and the fear of their nagging reproaches. The old Jewish proverb came to her mind: "The wolf is not afraid of the dog, but he hates his bark." "I'm not afraid of their black curses for sin. It's nothing to me if they accuse me of being an anti-Semite or a murderer, and yet why does it hurt me so?"

Rachel had prepared herself to face the usual hailstorm of reproaches and accusations, but as she entered the dark hallway of the tenement, she heard her father's voice chanting the old familiar Hebrew psalm of "The Race of Sorrows":

"Hear my prayer, O Lord, and let my cry come unto Thee.

For my days are consumed like smoke, and my bones are burned as an hearth.

I am like a pelican of the wilderness.

I am like an owl of the desert.

I have eaten ashes like bread and mingled my drink with weeping."

A faintness came over her. The sobbing strains of the lyric song melted into her veins like a magic sap, making her warm and human again. All her strength seemed to flow out of her in pity for her people. She longed to throw herself on the dirty, ill-smelling tenement stairs and weep: "Nothing is real but love—love. Nothing so false as ambition."

Since her early childhood she remembered often waking up in the middle of the night and hearing her father chant this age-old song of woe. There flashed before her a vivid picture of him, huddled in the corner beside the table piled high with Hebrew books, swaying to the rhythm of his Jeremiad, the sputtering light of the candle stuck in a bottle throwing uncanny shadows over his gaunt face. The skull-cap, the side-locks, and the long gray beard made him seem like some mystic stranger from a far-off world and not a father. The father of the daylight who ate with a knife, spat on the floor, and who was forever denouncing America and Americans was different from this mystic spirit stranger who could thrill with such impassioned rapture.

Thousands of years of exile, thousands of years of hunger, loneliness, and want swept over her as she listened to her father's voice. Something seemed to be crying out to her to run in and seize her father and mother in her arms and hold them close.

"Love, love—nothing is true between us but love," she thought.

But why couldn't she do what she longed to do? Why, with all her passionate sympathy for them, should any actual contact with her people seem so impossible? No, she couldn't go in just yet. Instead, she ran up on the roof, where she could be alone. She stationed herself at the air-shaft opposite their kitchen window, where for the first time since she had left in a rage she could see her old home.

Ach! what sickening disorder! In the sink were the dirty dishes stacked high, untouched, it looked, for days. The table still held the remains of the last meal. Clothes were strewn about the chairs. The bureau drawers were open, and their contents brimmed over in mad confusion.

"I couldn't endure it, this terrible dirt!" Her nails dug into her palms, shaking with the futility of her visit. "It would be worse than death to go back to them. It would mean giving up order, cleanliness, sanity, everything that I've striven all these years to attain. It would mean giving up the hope of my new world—the hope of Frank Baker."

The sound of the creaking door reached her where she crouched against the air-shaft. She looked again into the murky depths of the room. Her mother had entered. With arms full of paper bags of provisions, the old woman paused on the threshold, her eyes dwelling on the dim figure of her husband. A look of pathetic tenderness illumined her wrinkled features.

"I'll make something good to eat for you, yes?"

Reb Ravinsky only dropped his head on his breast. His eyes were red and dry, sandy with sorrow that could find no release in tears. Good God! Never had Rachel seen such profound despair. For the first time she noticed the grooved tracings of withering age knotted on his face and the growing hump on her mother's back.

"Already the shadow of death hangs over them," she thought as she watched them. "They're already with one foot in the grave. Why can't I be human to them before they're dead? Why can't I?"

Rachel blotted away the picture of the sordid room with both hands over her eyes.

"To death with my soul! I wish I were a plain human being with a heart instead of a monster of selfishness with a soul."

But the pity she felt for her parents began now to be swept away in a wave of pity for herself.

"How every step in advance costs me my heart's blood! My greatest tragedy in life is that I always see the two opposite sides at the same time. What seems to me right one day seems all wrong the next. Not only that, but many things seem right and wrong at the same time. I feel I have a right to my own life, and yet I feel just as strongly that I owe my father and mother something. Even if I don't love them, I have no right to step over them. I'm drawn to them by something more compelling than love. It is the cry of their dumb, wasted lives."

Again Rachel looked into the dimly lighted room below. Her mother placed food upon the table. With a self-effacing stoop of humility, she entreated, "Eat only while it is hot yet."

With his eyes fixed almost unknowingly, Reb Ravinsky sat down. Her mother took the chair opposite him, but she only pretended to eat the slender portion of the food she had given herself.

Rachel's heart swelled. Yes, it had always been like that. Her mother had taken the smallest portion of everything for herself. Complaints, reproaches, upbraidings, abuse, yes, all these had been heaped by her upon her mother; but always the juiciest piece of meat was placed on her plate, the thickest slice of bread; the warmest covering was given to her, while her mother shivered through the night.

"Ah, I don't want to abandon them!" she thought; "I only want to get to the place where I belong. I only want to get to the mountaintops and view the world from the heights, and then I'll give them everything I've achieved."

Her thoughts were sharply broken in upon by the loud sound of her father's eating. Bent over the table, he chewed with noisy gulps a piece of herring, his temples working to the motion of his jaws. With each audible swallow and smacking of the lips, Rachel's heart tightened with loathing.

"Their dirty ways turn all my pity into hate." She felt her toes and her fingers curl inward with disgust. "I'll never amount to anything if I'm not strong enough to break away from them once and for all." Hypnotizing herself into her line of self-defense, her thoughts raced on: "I'm only cruel to be kind. If I went back to them now, it would not be out of love, but because of weakness— because of doubt and unfaith in myself."

Rachel bluntly turned her back. Her head lifted. There was iron will in her jaws.

"If I haven't the strength to tear free from the old, I can never conquer the new. Every new step a man makes is a tearing away from those clinging to him. I must get tight and hard as rock inside of me if I'm ever to do the things I set out to do. I must learn to suffer and suffer, walk through blood and fire, and not bend from my course."

For the last time she looked at her parents. The terrible loneliness of their abandoned old age, their sorrowful eyes, the wrung-dry weariness on their faces, the whole black picture of her ruined, desolate home, burned into her flesh. She knew all the pain of one unjustly condemned, and the guilt of one with the spilt blood of helpless lives upon his hands. Then came tears, blinding, wrenching tears that tore at her heart until it seemed that they would rend her body into shreds.

"God! God!" she sobbed as she turned her head away from them, "if all this suffering were at least for something worth while, for something outside myself. But to have to break them and crush them merely be- cause I have a fastidious soul that can't stomach their table manners, merely because I can't strangle my aching ambitions to rise in the world!"

She could no longer sustain the conflict which raged within her higher and higher at every moment. With a sudden tension of all her nerves she pulled herself together and stumbled blindly downstairs and out of the house. And she felt as if she had torn away from the flesh and blood of her own body.

III

Out in the street she struggled to get hold of herself again. Despite the tumult and upheaval that racked her soul, an intoxicating lure still held her up—the hope of seeing Frank Baker that evening. She was indeed a storm-racked ship, but within sight of shore. She need but throw out the signal, and help was nigh. She need but confide to Frank Baker of her break with her people, and all the dormant sympathy between them would surge up. His understanding would widen and deepen because of her great need for his understanding. He would love her the more because of her great need for his love.

Forcing back her tears, stepping over her heartbreak, she hurried to the hotel where she was to meet him. Her father's impassioned rapture when he chanted the Psalms of David lit up the visionary face of the young Jewess.

"After all, love is the beginning of the real life," she thought as Frank Baker's dark, handsome face flashed before her. "With him to hold on to, I'll begin my new world."

Borne higher and higher by the intoxicating illusion of her great destiny, she cried:

"A person all alone is but a futile cry in an unheeding

wilderness. One alone is but a shadow, an echo of reality. It takes two together to create reality. Two together can pioneer a new world."

With a vision of herself and Frank Baker marching side by side to the conquest of her heart's desire, she added:

"No wonder a man's love means so little to the American woman. They belong to the world in which they are born. They belong to their fathers and mothers; they belong to their relatives and friends. They are human even without a man's love. I don't belong; I'm not human. Only a man's love can save me and make me human again."

It was the busy dinner-hour at the fashionable restaurant. Pausing at the doorway with searching eyes and lips eagerly parted, Rachel's swift glance circled the lobby. Those seated in the dining-room beyond who were not too absorbed in one another, noticed a slim, vivid figure of ardent youth, but with dark, age-old eyes that told of the restless seeking of her homeless race.

With nervous little movements of anxiety, Rachel sat down, got up, then started across the lobby. Half-way, she stopped, and her breath caught.

"Mr. Baker," she murmured, her hands fluttering toward him with famished eagerness. His smooth, athletic figure had a cock-sureness that to the girl's worshipping gaze seemed the perfection of male strength.

"You must be doing wonderful things," came from her admiringly, "you look so happy, so shining with life."

"Yes,"—he shook her hand vigorously,—"I've been living for the first time since I was a kid. I'm full of such interesting experiences. I'm actually working in an East Side settlement."

Dazed by his glamourous success, Rachel stammered

soft phrases of congratulations as he led her to a table. But seated opposite him, the face of this untried youth, flushed with the health and happiness of another world than that of the poverty-crushed Ghetto, struck her almost as an insincerity.

"You in an East Side settlement?" she interrupted sharply. "What reality can there be in that work for you?"

"Oh," he cried, his shoulders squaring with the assurance of his master's degree in sociology, "it's great to get under the surface and see how the other half lives. It's so picturesque! My conception of these people has greatly changed since I've been visiting their homes." He launched into a glowing account of the East Side as seen by a twenty-five-year-old college graduate.

"I thought them mostly immersed in hard labor, digging subways or slaving in sweatshops," he went on. "But think of the poetry which the immigrant is daily living!"

"But they're so sunk in the dirt of poverty, what poetry do you see there?"

"It's their beautiful home life, the poetic devotion between parents and children, the sacrifices they make for one another—"

"Beautiful home life? Sacrifices? Why, all I know of is the battle to the knife between parents and children. It's black tragedy that boils there, not the pretty sentiments that you imagine."

"My dear child,"—he waved aside her objection,— "you're too close to judge dispassionately. This very afternoon, on one of my friendly visits, I came upon a dear old man who peered up at me through horn-rimmed glasses behind his pile of Hebrew books. He was hardly able to speak English, but I found him a great scholar."

"Yes, a lazy old do-nothing, a bloodsucker on his wife and children."

Too shocked for remonstrance, Frank Baker stared at her.

"How else could he have time in the middle of the afternoon to pour over his books?" Rachel's voice was hard with bitterness. "Did you see his wife? I'll bet she was slaving for him in the kitchen. And his children slaving for him in the sweat-shop."

"Even so, think of the fine devotion that the women and children show in making the lives of your Hebrew scholars possible. It's a fine contribution to America, where our tendency is to forget idealism."

"Give me better a plain American man who supports his wife and children and I'll give you all those dreamers of the Talmud."

He smiled tolerantly at her vehemence.

"Nevertheless," he insisted, "I've found wonderful material for my new book in all this. I think I've got a new angle on the social types of your East Side."

An icy band tightened about her heart. "Social types," her lips formed. How could she possibly confide to this man of the terrible tragedy that she had been through that very day? Instead of the understanding and sympathy that she had hoped to find, there were only smooth platitudes, the sightseer's surface interest in curious "social types."

Frank Baker talked on. Rachel seemed to be listening, but her eyes had a far-off, abstracted look. She was quiet as a spinning-top is quiet, her thoughts and emotions revolving within her at high speed.

"That man in love with me? Why, he doesn't see me or feel me. I don't exist to him. He's only stuck on himself, blowing his own horn. Will he never stop with his 'I,' 'I,' 'I,'? Why, I was a crazy lunatic to think that just because we took the same courses in college, he would understand me out in the real world."

All the fire suddenly went out of her eyes. She looked a thousand years old as she sank back wearily in her chair.

"Oh, but I'm boring you with all my heavy talk on sociology." Frank Baker's words seemed to come to her from afar. "I have tickets for a fine musical comedy that will cheer you up, Miss Ravinsky—"

"Thanks, thanks," she cut in hurriedly. Spend a whole evening sitting beside him in a theater when her heart was breaking? No. All she wanted was to get away—away where she could be alone. "I have work to do," she heard herself say. "I've got to get home."

Frank Baker murmured words of polite disappointment and escorted her back to her door. She watched the sure swing of his athletic figure as he strode away down the street, then she rushed upstairs.

Back in her little room, stunned, bewildered, blinded with her disillusion, she sat staring at her four empty walls.

Hours passed, but she made no move, she uttered no sound. Doubled fists thrust between her knees, she sat there, staring blindly at her empty walls.

"I can't live with the old world, and I'm yet too green for the new. I don't belong to those who gave me birth or to those with whom I was educated."

Was this to be the end of all her struggles to rise in America, she asked herself, this crushing daze of loneliness? Her driving thirst for an education, her desperate battle for a little cleanliness, for a breath of beauty, the tearing away from her own flesh and blood to free herself from the yoke of her parents—what was it all worth now? Where did it lead to? Was loneliness to be the fruit of it all?

Night was melting away like a fog; through the open

window the first lights of dawn were appearing. Rachel felt the sudden touch of the sun upon her face, which was bathed in tears. Overcome by her sorrow, she shuddered and put her hand over her eyes as tho to shut out the unwelcome contact. But the light shone through her fingers.

Despite her weariness, the renewing breath of the fresh morning entered her heart like a sunbeam. A mad longing for life filled her veins.

"I want to live," her youth cried. "I want to live, even at the worst."

Live how? Live for what? She did not know. She only felt she must struggle against her loneliness and weariness as she had once struggled against dirt, against the squalor and ugliness of her Ghetto home.

Turning from the window, she concentrated her mind, her poor tired mind, on one idea.

"I have broken away from the old world; I'm through with it. It's already behind me. I must face this loneliness till I get to the new world. Frank Baker can't help me; I must hope for no help from the outside. I'm alone; I'm alone till I get there.

"But am I really alone in my seeking? I'm one of the millions of immigrant children, children of loneliness, wandering between worlds that are at once too old and too new to live in."

Hester Street

I paused in front of my rooming house on Hester Street. This was 1920, when Hester Street was the pushcart center of the East Side. The air reeked with the smell of fish and overripe fruit from the carts in front of the house. I peeked into the basement window. The landlady was not there to nag me for the rent. I crept into her kitchen, filled my pitcher with water and hurried out. In my room I set the kettle boiling. There wasn't much taste to the stale tea leaves but the hot water warmed me. I was still sipping my tea, thankful for this short reprieve from my landlady, when I heard my name shouted outside the door.

The angel of death, I thought, my landlady had come to put me out! And Hester Street had gathered to watch another eviction. I opened the door with fear.

Mrs. Katz with her baby in her arms, Mrs. Rubin drying her wet hands on her apron, and Zalmon Shlomoh, the fish peddler, crowded into my room, pushing forward a Western Union messenger who handed me a yellow envelope.

"*Oi-oi weh!* A telegram!" Mrs. Rubin wailed. "Somebody died?"

Their eyes gleamed with prying curiosity. "Read—read already!" they clamored.

I ripped open the envelope and read:

TELEPHONE IMMEDIATELY FOR AN APPOINT-
MENT TO DISCUSS MOTION PICTURE RIGHTS
OF "HUNGRY HEARTS"

R.L. GIFFEN

"Who died?" they demanded.

"Nobody died. It's only a place for a job," I said, shooing them out of the room.

I reread the message. "Telephone immediately!" It was from one of the big moving-picture agents. In those days Hollywood was still busy with Westerns and Polly-anna romances. The studios seldom bought stories from life. This was like winning a ticket on a lottery.

Hungry Hearts had been my first book. It had been praised by the critics, esteemed as literature. That meant it didn't sell. After spending the two hundred dollars I had received in royalties, I was even poorer than when I had started writing.

And now movie rights! Money! Wealth! I could get the world for the price of a telephone call. But if I had had a nickel for a telephone I wouldn't have fooled a starving stomach with stewed-over tea leaves. I needed a nickel for telephoning, ten cents for carfare—fifteen cents! What could I pawn to get fifteen cents?

I looked about my room. The rickety cot didn't belong to me. The rusty gas plate on the window sill? My type-writer? The trunk that was my table? Then I saw the shawl, my mother's shawl that served as a blanket and a cover for my cot.

Nobody in our village in Poland had had a shawl like it. It had been Mother's wedding present from her rich uncle in Warsaw. It had been her Sabbath, her holiday. ... When she put it on she outshone all the other women on the way to the synagogue.

Old and worn—it held memories of my childhood, put space and color in my drab little room. It redeemed the squalor in which I had to live. But this might be the last time I'd have to pawn it. I seized the shawl and rushed with it to the pawnshop.

Zaretzky, the pawnbroker, was a bald-headed dwarf, grown gray with the years in the dark basement—tight-skinned and crooked from squeezing pennies out of despairing people.

I watched his dirty, bony fingers appraise the shawl. "An old rag!" he grunted, peering at me through his thick-rimmed glasses. He had always intimidated me before, but this time the telegram in my hand made me bold.

"See here, Zaretzky," I said, "this shawl is rarer than diamonds—an antique from Poland, pure wool. The older it gets, the finer—the softer the colors—"

He spread it out and held it up to the light. "A moth-eaten rag full of holes!"

"You talk as if I were a new customer. You make nothing of the best things. As you did with my samovar."

"A samovar is yet something. But this!" He pushed the shawl from him. "A quarter. Take it or leave it."

"This was the finest shawl in Plinsk. It's hand-woven, hand-dyed. People's lives are woven into it."

"For what is past nobody pays. Now it's junk—falling apart."

"I'm only asking a dollar. It's worth ten times that much. Only a dollar!"

"A quarter. You want it? Yes or no?"

I grabbed the quarter and fled.

Within a half-hour I was at the agent's office.

"I've great news for you," he said, drawing up a chair near his desk. "I've practically sold your book to Hollywood. Goldwyn wants it. Fox is making offers, too, but I think Goldwyn is our best bet. They offered five thousand dollars. I'm holding out for ten."

I had pawned Mother's shawl to get there, and this man talked of thousands of dollars. Five, ten thousand dollars was a fortune in 1920. I was suddenly aware of my hunger. I saw myself biting into thick, juicy steaks, dipping fresh rolls into mounds of butter, swallowing whole platters of French fried potatoes in one gulp.

"If we settle with Goldwyn," Mr. Giffen said, "he will want you to go to Hollywood to collaborate on the script."

I stood up to go, dizzy from lack of food and so much excitement.

"Maybe what you're saying is real," I said. "If it is, then can you advance me one dollar on all these thousands?"

Smiling, he handed me a bill.

I walked out of his office staring at the ten-dollar bill in my hand. Directly across the street was the white-tiled front of a Child's restaurant. How often I had stood outside this same restaurant, watching the waitresses clear away leftover food and wanting to cry out, "Don't throw it away! Give it to me. I'm hungry!" I stumbled through the door, sank into the first vacant chair and ordered the most expensive steak on the menu. A platter was set before me — porterhouse steak, onions, potatoes, rolls, butter. I couldn't eat fast enough. Before I was half through, my throat tightened. My head bent over my plate, tears rolled down my cheeks onto the uneaten food.

When I hadn't had a penny for a roll I had had the appetite of a wolf that could devour the earth. Now that I could treat myself to a dollar dinner, I couldn't take another bite. But just having something to eat, even though I could only half eat it, made me see the world with new eyes. If only Father and Mother were alive now! How I longed to be at peace with them!

I had not meant to abandon them when I left home—

I had only wanted to get to the place where I belonged. To do it, I had to strike out alone.

If my mother could only have lived long enough to see that I was not the heartless creature I seemed to be! As for my father—would he forgive me even now?

Now that there was no longer reason to feel sorry for myself, my self-pity turned to regret for all that I did not do and might have done for them.

The waitress started to remove the dishes.

"I'm not through!" I held onto the plate, still starved for the steak and potatoes I could not eat. The agent's talk of Hollywood might have been only a dream. But steak was real. When no one was looking, I took out my handkerchief, thrust the meat and cold potatoes into it, covered it with my newspaper and sneaked out like a thief with the food for which I had paid.

Back in my room I opened the newspaper bundle, still too excited with the prospect of Hollywood to be able to eat. "God! What a hoarding creature I've become!" I cried out in self-disgust. In my purse was the change from the ten-dollar bill the agent had given me. More than enough for a dozen meals. And yet the hoarding habit of poverty was so deep in my bones that I had to bring home the food that I could not eat.

I leaned out of the window. Lily, the alley cat, was scavenging the garbage can as usual. I had named her Lily because she had nothing but garbage to eat and yet somehow looked white and beautiful like the lilies that rise out of dunghills.

"Lily!" I called to her, holding up the steak. The next moment she bounded up on my window sill, devouring the steak and potatoes in huge gulps.

"I've been a pauper all my life," I told Lily as I watched her eat. "But I'll be a pauper no longer. I'll have money, plenty of it. I'll not only have money to buy food when I'm hungry, but I'll have men who'll love me on my terms. An end to hoarding food, or hoarding love!"

I threw open the trunk, dug down and yanked out the box of John Morrow's letters, determined to tear them up and shed the memory of them once and for all. For years those letters had been to me music and poetry. I had stayed up nights to console my loneliness reading and rereading them, drugged with the opiate of his words.

But now, with the prospect of Hollywood, I began to hate those letters. Why hang on to words when the love that had inspired them was dead? In Hollywood there would be new people. There would be other men.

I seized the first letter and began tearing it. But a panicky fear of loss stopped me. Money could buy meat and mink, rye bread and rubies, but not the beauty of his words. Those letters were my assurance that I was a woman who could love and be loved. Without them, I was again the oddity of Hester Street, an object of pity and laughter.

"Poor thing! I can't stand the starved-dog look in her eyes," I had overheard one of the men in the shop say to another.

"Well, if you're so sorry for her, marry her," came the jeering retort.

"Marry her? Oi-i-i! Oi-yoi! That *meshugeneh?* That redheaded witch? Her head is on wheels, riding on air. She's not a woman. She has a *dybbuk,* a devil, a book for a heart."

But when I met John Morrow, the *dybbuk* that drove away other men had drawn him to me. He saw my people in me, struggling for a voice. I could no more tear up those letters than I could root out the memory of him!

I slipped the torn pieces of the letter into the envelope, put it back with the others in the box and stuck it at the bottom of my trunk, under my old clothes.

A week later Mr. Giffen asked me to lunch to talk over the movie contract I was to sign.

After I had signed a twenty-page contract, Giffen handed me a check—a check made out to me—a check for nine thousand dollars.

I've deducted one thousand for my ten per cent," he explained.

I looked at the check. Nine thousand dollars!

"Riches for a lifetime!" I cried.

Giffen smiled. "It's only the beginning. When you're in Hollywood you'll see the more you have, the more you'll get."

He took out my railroad reservation from his wallet and handed it to me. "They want you to assist in the production of the book. You're to get two hundred a week and all your expenses while there."

He gave me another check for a hundred dollars. "This is for your incidentals on the train. Meals for three and a half days—one hundred dollars. Not so bad!" He patted my hand. "Young lady! You go on salary the moment you step on the train."

I told him I could be ready as soon as I got something out of a pawnshop.

With my purse full of money, I hurried to Zaretzky's to redeem my shawl.

"Zaretzky!" I charged into the basement. "I forgot to take my receipt for the shawl!"

"Forgot, nothing! I gave it to you in your hand."

"I swear to you, I left it on the counter."

"If you were crazy enough to lose it, it's not my fault."

I took out a five-dollar bill. "Here's five dollars for your quarter," I said. "What more do you want?"

He made no move. He stood like stone staring at me.

"Shylock! Here's ten dollars! I have no time to bargain with you. If that's not enough, here's twice ten dollars! Twenty dollars for your twenty-five cents!"

There was a flicker in the black pinpoints of his eyes. He took out a signed receipt from the money box. "I sold it the day you brought it here for five dollars," he groaned, his face distorted by frustrated greed.

The next day I packed my belongings without the shawl that had gone with me everywhere I went. The loss of that one beautiful thing which all my money could not reclaim shadowed my prospective trip to Hollywood.

The distrust of good fortune always in the marrow of my bones made me think of my father. While I was struggling with hunger and want, trying to write, I feared to go near him. I couldn't stand his condemnation of my lawless, godless, selfish existence. But now, with Hollywood ahead of me, I had the courage to face him. As I entered the dark hallway of the tenement where he lived, I heard his voice chanting.

"And a man shall be as a hiding place from the wind, and covert from the tempest; as rivers of water in a dry place, as the shadow of a great rock in a weary land . . ."

Since earliest childhood I had heard this chant of Isaiah. It was as familiar to me as Mother Goose rhymes to other children. Hearing it again after so many years, I was struck for the first time by the beauty of the words. Though my father was poor and had nothing, the Torah, the poetry of prophets, was his daily bread.

He was still chanting as I entered, a gray-bearded man in a black skullcap.

"And the eyes of them that see shall not be dim, and the ears of them that hear shall hearken. The heart of the rash shall understand knowledge, and the tongue of the stammerers shall be ready to speak plainly..."

As I stood there, waiting for him to see me, I noticed the aging stoop of his shoulders. He was getting paler, thinner. The frail body accused me for having been away so long. But in the same moment of guilt the smells of the musty room in which he wouldn't permit a window to be opened or a book to be dusted made me want to run. On the table piled high with his papers and dust-laden books were dishes with remains of his last meal— cabbage soup and pumpernickel. He was as unaware of the squalor around him as a medieval monk.

Dimly I realized that this new world didn't want his kind. He had no choice but to live for God. And I, his daughter, who abandoned him for the things of this world, had joined the world against him.

He looked up and saw me.

"So you've come at last? You've come to see your old father?"

"I was so busy...." I mumbled. And then, hastily, to halt his reproaches, I reached into my bag and dropped ten ten-dollar bills on the open page of his book. He pushed aside the bills as if they would contaminate the holiness of the script.

"Months, almost a year, you've been away...."

"Bessie, Fannie live right near here, they promised to look after you...."

"They have their own husbands to look after. You're my only unmarried daughter. Your first duty to God is to serve your father. But what's an old father to an *Amerikanerin,* a daughter of Babylon?"

"Your daughter of Babylon brought you a hundred dollars."

"Can your money make up for your duty as a daughter? In America, money takes the place of God."

"But I earned that money with my writing." For all his scorn of my godlessness, I thought he would take a father's pride in my success. "Ten thousand they paid me...."

He wouldn't let me finish. He shook a warning finger in my face. "Can you touch pitch without being defiled? Neither can you hold on to all that money without losing your soul."

Even in the street, his words still rang in my ears. "Daughter of Babylon! You've polluted your inheritance .... You'll wander in darkness and none shall be there to save you...."

His old God could not save me in a new world, I told myself. Why did we come to America, if not to achieve all that had been denied us for centuries in Europe? Fear and poverty were behind me. I was going into a new world of plenty. I would learn to live in the now...not in the next world.

I had but to open my purse, look at my reservation for a drawing room on the fastest flyer to Hollywood, think of the fabulous salary I was to be paid even while traveling, and no hope in which I might indulge was too high, no longing too visionary.

Grand Central Station, where I waited for my train, seemed an unreal place. Within the vast marble structure people rushed in and out, meeting, parting and hurrying on, each in pursuit of his own dream. As I stood lost in my thoughts, every man I saw seemed John Morrow coming to see me off. If so incredible a thing could happen as my going to Hollywood, surely John Morrow could appear. He must know *Hungry Hearts* was written for him. He must sense my need to share my wealth with him even more than I had needed him in poverty.

The gates opened. My train was called. I picked up my bundle, started through the gate, still looking back, still expecting the miracle. I could not give up the hope that love as great as his had been could ever cease.

The first days and nights on the train I was too dazed by the sudden turn of events to notice the view from my window. Miles of beautiful country I saw, unaware of what I was seeing. Then one morning I woke up and saw the desert stretching out on both sides. The train raced through the wide monotonous landscape at a terrific pace to reach its destination on scheduled time.

It was getting hotter and hotter. Sand sifted through the screened air vents and closed doors. The train stopped at the station to refuel. Passengers stepped out to buy trinkets from the Indians squatting on the platform. Over the entrance of an adobe building I read in gilt letters the inscription:

> THE DESERT WAITED, SILENT AND HOT
> AND FIERCE IN ITS DESOLATION, HOLDING
> ITS TREASURES UNDER SEAL OF DEATH
> AGAINST THE COMING OF THE STRONG
> ONE.

I looked across the vast space and thought of the time when all this silent sand was a rolling ocean. What eons had to pass for the ocean to dry into this arid waste! In the immensity of the desert the whirl of trivialities which I had so magnified all fell away. I was suspended in timelessness—sand, sky, and space. What a relief it was to let go—not to think—not to feel, but rest, silent—past, present and future stretching to infinity.

Slowly, imperceptibly, the dry desert air receded before the humid, subtropical warmth of southern California. The sense of time and the concern with self stirred again. Green hills, dazzling gardens and orange groves, towering date palms ushered in the great adventure ahead of me.

Important People

Leaning against the cushions of the car that was taking me to the home of Rupert Hughes, I caught sight of my straggling hair in the mirror. I smoothed it back as best I could. I looked down at my plain blue serge skirt, my thick-soled sandals. Why had I never dressed like other women? It wasn't just a matter of being poor. The poorest shopgirl with her mind on style managed to look as smart as other shopgirls. I never could or would fit into the up-to-date clothes that everybody else wore. Even now when I no longer had to search through bargain basements, now that I had money enough to shop at the best stores, perversity made me cling to my pushcart clothes. Even in Hollywood I wanted to be myself— whatever that was.

But you're no longer scrubbing floors or punching a machine, I told myself. You're on your way to meet who's who in Hollywood, about to be initiated into the sacred circle of "eminent authors." I looked at my hands, bitten with the sharp red and gray of work. Why didn't you celebrate the great event, treat yourself to a manicure? Do you have to look like a *yenteh* from Hester Street to be yourself?

Immediately the other side of me protested. What's wrong with looking like Hester Street? I am Hester Street. Why should I be afraid to be what I am? Why should I dress up to meet them? Would they dress down to meet me? The familiar feel of the creases in my blouse, my unpolished shoes, the shine of my old skirt reassured me that with all the change around me, I was still unchanged. I was still myself.

But can you be yourself with the money from the movies tucked safely in the bank? You're afraid to spend your money and you're afraid to give it up. You're afraid to plunge back into the poverty and dirt from which money has saved you. Yet you fear what money may do to you. You want to be a person of importance. You want to be a success—and yet you can't give up what you were when you were nobody. You want too much.

The sun was beginning to set, weaving circles of light over the tall Hawaiian pines of Beverly Hills. Never had I seen skies so blue, grass so green. The toy houses and fairylike gardens that I glimpsed as the car sped along added a fantastic setting to my dreams of the fellowship of writers.

The chauffeur turned the car up a graveled drive lined with exotic trees and shrubs. He stopped before a villa as plain as a New England farmhouse.

I walked up to the porch, and then paused in sudden doubt of myself. All my instincts cried: Don't! Don't go in! Run! Make your escape before any one sees you. You don't belong here.

But this was my first chance to see the other world. Even if it killed me, I had to see, I had to know what it was like. I hid behind a rosebush and looked in. Men in tails and women in low-necked evening gowns stood around talking.

I recognized Will Rogers, Elinor Glyn, Gertrude Atherton, Katharine Newlin Burt, Alice Duer Miller. I had seen their pictures in the Sunday papers, authors of the latest best sellers, their names printed in big letters on the covers of popular magazines.

The makers of best sellers! Fear and awe of success fought within me. To my frightened eyes the authors in that drawing room looked like conquering gods towering over me. Who was I to have ventured among them? One book, and only a pitiful tale of myself at that—A writer? Never had I felt so hopelessly out of place.

"You don't own the dirt under their doorsteps." Words with which my mother had crushed the courage out of me as a child rushed over me, barring that door.

They had invited me. They had made the overtures. I tried to reason, but it was no use. I could not bridge the gap between myself and the celebrities in that drawing room.

I turned to flee just as Rupert Hughes opened the door.

"We've been waiting for you. And here you are, standing us up—"

"I was scared to come in!"

He put his arm around me and laughed as a grownup laughs at a child. His easy, affable smile melted the arrogance with which I had armed myself when I started out in my old clothes. They told me he was the richest, the most versatile of the Hollywood authors. He was a musician, a journalist, a historian, and movie producer. And yet, none of the airs of the big shot about him. He was a short, solidly built man, his head close to his heart.

"I'd like you to meet my wife," he said, introducing a slender, dark-haired woman.

"So glad to have you with us." She smiled, her glance sweeping over me in swift appraisal.

As in a dream, I was aware of some one taking my hand and guiding me to the foyer where a maid helped me take off my hat and coat. And then I stepped on a carpet of air, into a room of dim, golden light. Faces gleamed to me out of the shadows, luminous, ephemeral. Where had I seen this visionary place before? I had seen it when I was in the dark hold of the steerage, on the way to America, when I was sewing buttons in a factory, when I walked the streets trying to feed my hunger with dreams of my rise in the world.

"How do you like Hollywood?" some one asked.

"It's so different," I said, shocked by the shrillness of my voice. "There was a freezing blizzard when I left New York. And when I got here, I walked into sunshine and flowers. It's all so unreal. . . ."

"We New Yorkers think no place is real but New York," Alice Duer Miller said with her warm smile.

"We New Yorkers!" She was including me in her circle, treating me as if I belonged to it! If I could only tell her what it meant to be among fellow writers who understood all I was trying to be!

Release from fear and anxiety spread a healing glow of good will in me toward all these lovely, important people. My lifelong hatred for the rich, the successful, turned to servile gratitude for their friendliness. In my eagerness to become like them, with the ardor of a convert to a new faith, I repudiated all that I had been. The poor, I thought, were too submerged in the fight for bread to indulge in the amenities of life. Success made people kinder, nobler, more beautiful. Only the rich had the leisure, the peace of mind to take an interest in one another.

I could almost feel my father turn in his grave in horror at my apostasy. His own daughter losing her soul for a rich woman's smile! I could almost see him step into the drawing room and shake a warning finger at me. "Can fire and water be together? Neither can godliness and ease."

Your godliness is for the dying, the renegade in me retorted. I'm young. I'm going to have all that the poor never had. I'll be at ease in Zion. I'll have riches, fame, success—all the fullness of the earth—and heaven too.

I took up a glass of sherry and swallowed all of it. The pleasant warmth of the drink gave me the courage to look around. My hand ran over the arm of my chair to feel the texture of the fabric. The rug on the floor, the paintings on the wall, the mellow lights of the lamps—colors and lines of everything flowed into one another. Flowers on old mahogany, long-stemmed glasses on silver trays, perfumes blending with cigarette smoke. But what bewitched me most was the gaiety of these people, the ease with which they enjoyed the moment, as if it would last forever.

I turned to Mrs. Miller standing beside me. "I read your last story in the *Post*," I said. "You have such velvet smoothness of style. When you write, it's as if you sat back in an easy chair in the front parlor of your mind, where everything is in perfect order."

She smiled away my enthusiasm. "I've been a mathematics teacher. Mathematics has given me a sense of proportion. When I write, the plot comes out complete like a baby out of its mother's womb."

"Oh! How I envy your clarity!" I said. "And the ease with which you turn out one novel after another. I never know what I'm trying to write until it's written. Then begins the labor of cutting to clarify the meaning. I never know whether what I cut out isn't better than what I left in—"

"Every writer has to find his own way of working. I think out every word of my novels before I begin. Then I type them with practically no revisions."

No revisions! I stared at her, trying to imagine what life would be like without wrestling with each living word.

"The trouble with me," said Elinor Glyn, "my plots

come spinning so fast I don't take time to develop the characters."

I turned from her to Rupert Hughes. "Can you shake your stories out of your sleeve too?"

"My plots don't spin at all." He laughed. "How about you, Miss Yezierska?"

"I can never learn to plot or plan. It's always a mystery to me how I ever work out a beginning or an end of a story."

My glass refilled, I gulped it down, forgetting I was not drinking water, and went on talking. People from other parts of the room came over. The little common sense left in the back of my head cried: Stop! Don't make a fool of yourself. Don't walk out naked for these people.

But the words kept coming. "I only want to take the hurt out of my heart when I write. But the minute my pencil touches paper, I begin to worry how to write instead of going ahead and writing. And I become stiff and self-conscious. Is it the fear of being a foreigner that makes me want to explain myself so much? But I've had moments when I was so filled with the life I've lived I felt myself flow out into my words. These rare moments when I was my real self, I took back the fraud, the humbug, like God absolving the Prodigal."

Rupert Hughes took my arm and led the way into the dining room. We seated ourselves around a table gleaming with silver and fine linen. For once in my life I was where I wanted to be. For once I was part of everything. It was all I could do not to let my head sink on the table and weep. I wanted to weep and I wanted to clap my hands and sing and shout. "I've arrived! I'm in with Hollywood royalty! Behold! Pushcart clothes and all—I am the guest of honor at the feast!"

The table reeling, dancing a jig, champagne floating

in foam, roast squabs with lace-paper frills on their legs — and me in my old clothes, the star of the evening — that's America.

"What are you thinking of?" Mr. Hughes asked.

"Ask me when I'm sober."

"Why be sober?" And he motioned the waiter to re-fill my glass with champagne.

"How's your picture going?" Mrs. Hughes asked.

"It's going to be the greatest picture of the century." I heard myself repeat Paul Bern's boast. "The *Uncle Tom's Cabin* of the immigrant."

"Have another drink," someone said. "If you have enough champagne you'll believe anything they tell you."

I noticed Alice Duer Miller smiling across the table. Was she laughing at me? Her smile made me suddenly feel the gulf between us. And now, beginning to doubt again, my ears caught snatches of conversation that widened and deepened that gulf.

"When I sell the movie rights, I get all the money I can out of them, and never bother to see the picture...."

"Only the title of my last book was used. I can sell it again — change names of the characters — change the setting...."

"Royalties? Poison ivy. Don't touch it. Get all you can get. But get it in cash. Sign anything they give you. What's the difference? Contracts don't mean a thing...."

"I wasn't the first to cash in on the gold rush in Alaska. But I had the goods when the market was soaring. I knew Alaska and had facts to boost my fiction."

I pushed the empty wine glass from me. I had dreamed of Olympian gods and woke up among hucksters. I remembered seeing Shakespeare's *Merchant of Venice* in modern dress. Now I saw the fish market in evening clothes. The fight that went on at the pushcarts in Hester Street went on in this Hollywood drawing room.

Loneliness oppressed me. Even if I turned myself inside out, I could not compete with the sharp, shrewd barter of those business authors. If I could not stand haggling and bargaining for pennies at the pushcarts, how could I stand this movie market where the bargaining for contracts and royalties was multiplied into fabulous thousands of dollars?

When some of the guests were beginning to leave, I went for my hat and coat. Will Rogers stopped me. "See here, gal! Can I give you a lift home?"

I looked at his farmer's sunburned face with the funny flop of hair hanging over his forehead, his laughing eyes.

"How does all this fuss and feathers hit you, sister?" he asked, putting his hand on my shoulder.

"Is this Hollywood's Four Hundred?" I asked. Then, noticing his blue flannel shirt, I shook a finger at him. "You, too, dared to crash into society without evening clothes?"

His laughter was as refreshing as sunlight and mountain air. I laughed with him as I never had before.

"Come on, gal! I can't say your name." He took my arm and led me to his car.

My Last Hollywood Script

I stood in a huge hall, between the president of the university and the president of the sorority, shaking hands. An endless double line of faces smiled up at me, hands reached out to clasp my hand. The gleaming lights of the great hall dazzled me, and still more dazzling were the young girls dressed as if for a ball in low-necked evening gowns. The blue wool dress I wore looked like sackcloth against the colorful chiffons and silks of my audience.

I thought of the days when I had watched from the side lines of a theater. Those gowns had always been to me the symbol of another world. I had never had an evening gown. Now that I could afford to buy one, I felt I was too old to wear it.

A wave of self-pity drowned out my stage fright. I wanted to bury my face in my hands and weep because I had never been young and beautiful like the girls who were coming up now to shake my hand.

I looked at these lovely creatures floating on the surface of life. The joy of youth glowed in their faces. Homes sheltered them from what went on in the world. They were born into the good things of life—education, clothes, friends. The give and take of love was as natural to them as breathing.

The room sang with their gay young voices until the signal came to file into the banquet hall. With the solemnity of a ritual, the president led me to my place at the center table. An elaborate dinner was served, but I could not eat. I kept glancing at the notes in my hand, rehearsing my speech. I had learned it by heart, but the words were slipping away, my mind turning blank. What a fool I was to have come here, only to expose my ignorance, my terror of strangers!

All at once I became aware of eyes. Hungry young eyes boring into me. Eyes filled with blind faith, crying for miracles. Eyes like X-rays peering into me to discover the formula for quick success, the touchstone for becoming famous overnight. Eyes, all prayer and pleading: How can we conquer the world? Tell us your secret.

These lucky young girls—envying me! They didn't even know how happy they were. Everything the world could give was theirs—and yet they wanted something from me! What had I to give them? Hunger? Homelessness? The brutal fight to make my way?

Suddenly I hated them. They, who had everything, now wanted to wrest from me they knew not what. I'd give it to them. I'd give them a whiff of Hester Street.

Without waiting for the chairman to introduce me, I stood up and plunged right in. "I have here, in my hands the few words I had prepared to say to you. It was written before I looked into your eyes. There's something in your eyes that tells me you don't want speeches. You don't want the fairy tale, the success story of the movies. You deserve the truth.

"I feel as if I had started writing a story and then had to scrap everything I had written. Your eyes are giving me courage to tell you the truth."

Such swift response rushed to me out of their eyes! I felt like a parent, arm upraised to strike an errant child —shamed by the wide, trusting look of innocence. Something opened between us that made me talk as if I had always known them. In the past whenever I spoke to an audience, my voice had sounded like a ventriloquist's dummy. But now my voice flowed with an ease I had never experienced.

"What is your conception of success? My idea of success is to be wholly myself. I was always afraid to be myself. This is the first time I have faced an audience without fear.

"Look! I'm tearing up my prepared speech—my last Hollywood script." I tossed the pieces into the air like a bunch of confetti. "Isn't it wonderful—just to be yourself! And you can only be yourself when among friends. We're just people, drawn to one another at sight, swapping experiences. Write out any questions you want to ask me on the back of your menu cards."

And so while dinner was served, the questions were passed up to me. It was such a relief to have said those few words I could even swallow a few sips of soup before I stood up again to real aloud the first question: *"What helped you most to become a writer?"*

"My greatest stimulus to writing was the teacher who said, 'There are too many writers and too few cooks,' and advised me to stick to the job that assured me a living. I told him if I had to spend my life cooking for a living, that would be existing, not living.

"He said to me, 'Even if you learned to write what you want to write, who would read it? Where would you sell it? There's no market for your stuff. People aren't interested in the immigrant, in poverty, in suffering. They want to be entertained. They need cheering up. Your stuff lacks humor. It's too full of gloom. People read to escape from their troubles. They want glamour, romance. Read the popular magazines. Read what successful authors are writing.'

"'But why should I copy other authors when I have something of my own to write?" I asked him.

"It was his practical formula for popular magazine success which drove me to defy all sound advice—all reason and common sense—to forsake family, friends, do without sleep, without clothes, withdraw from the world, from life itself—to write. But it was not long before I discovered that a writer cannot withdraw from life and go on writing, any more than a candle can burn without oxygen."

There were many such questions that I answered briefly, but one was a challenge that took up most of the evening. *"You said in a newspaper interview that the things which could not kill you were the making of you. What things did you mean?"*

"There were so many things that crushed the life out of me, so many ways of dying. Every step of the way up in my writing career was enough to kill me if I had not been stronger than death. Take this, for instance:

"After I sold my first story for twenty-five dollars, I gave up my job and decided to live or die by my writing. The twenty-five dollars were soon used up. I was in the throes of my second story, and I was starving. I went to my sister. She had nine children. They never had enough to eat, but occasionally they let me have a bite from the little they had. The children were in the street when I arrived and my sister was next door at a neighbor's. My sister's house was always open. Poor people have no need to lock their homes. A pot of oatmeal was boiling on the stove. I seized the pot, rushed with it to the sink, added a little cold water to cool it and began wolfing it. That whole pot of oatmeal only whetted my hunger. There was a loaf of bread in the breadbox. Just as I started to break off a piece the children stormed in, and seeing me at their bread, tore it out of my hands. At this point my sister returned, saw the empty pot. Her shriek raised the roof of the flat.

"She threw up her hands, screaming, 'You're a wild animal—'

"'I was so hungry—'

"'*You* were hungry? What about the children?'

"'I don't live for myself—'

"'For what do you live?'

"'For my writing—'

"'A writer she wants to be yet! A crazy animal that's what you are. Stealing bread from starving children—that's worse than stealing pennies from a blind man's cup—'

"'A mother has a right to steal to feed a hungry child. I have a right to steal to finish my story—'

"'Who gives you the right? Your craziness gives you the right?'

"'All right, then, I'm crazy. I'm a thief, a criminal. Call a policeman!' I shouted above the yells of the children. 'Say I've robbed. If it's a crime to want to give your thoughts to the world, then I'm a criminal. Send me to prison. I'll have something to eat till I finish my story. Some of the greatest books in the world were written in prison. Call the police. Let them lock me up.'

"I wish I could still justify the stealing of that oatmeal as I was able to fifteen years ago. But every step of my writing career was a brutal fight, like the stealing of that oatmeal from hungry children."

Even the waiters stopped removing plates and stood with the trays in their hands, listening openmouthed. One confession led to another.

"When I banked the money the movies paid me for *Hungry Hearts,* the elation of suddenly possessing a fortune was overshadowed by the voice of conscience: What is the difference between a potbellied boss who exploits the labor of helpless workers and an author who grows rich writing of the poor?"

When the applause came I felt as if I had walked out of darkness into light. Those young girls had struck the dead rock of frustration I had carried in my heart—and the living waters of life began to flow again.

There was something to being famous after all, I rejoiced. If I were a nobody, they would never have listened to me. They think I'm a success, and so my opinion is respected. I gave them something to think about.

But when they came crowding around me, murmuring, "It was so nice!" "So interesting!" "We'll never forget this thrilling evening!" the wonderful moment of exaltation, when I felt at one with my audience, began to fade. Had it been only a fairy tale to them? Instead of showing them the barren road of my success, had I only sharpened their desire for it? In their shining eyes I saw the hunger for recognition at any price—their lust and mine for the glory of the limelight—the boom of the crowd that pursues a celebrity. Had my efforts to tell my story ended again in failure?

Another girl came up. "You're wonderful!" She shook my hand. "I only wish I had known you when you were poor and obscure."

I looked at her bright young face, surprised to see that it was already marked by anxiety.

"I'm working my way through college," she said. "I've been on my own since twelve."

She was so pretty! How could she have known poverty and look so gay, so decorative?

I turned to the other girls around me, my feeling of righteousness begging to crumble. Just because they had never been starved enough to steal bread from hungry children, I had condemned them as callous and frivolous. The truth with which I wanted to shock them had been only the vanity of the injured showing off scars.

I had erected a wall of self-defense around me and shot arrows of envy at them. Immune to envy, immune to criticism, they swept across the wall and conquered me.

All at once I loved them. As I had made a bunch of confetti from my prepared speech, so I would have gladly made a bonfire of everything I had to feed the flame of their trusting youth.

Bread and Wine in the Wilderness

The Writer's Project became more desolate after Jeremiah's death. Every day it became harder to blind ourselves to the cold fact that we, like the privy-builders and road-makers of other public projects, were being paid not for what we did, but to put money into circulation. For right next to the supervisors who handed us our assignments were the desks of the new rewrite men who were actually turning out the *Guide.*

Newspapers clamored for the end of "boondoggling." And our director, frightened by the clamor, issued commands for more efficiency. The supervisors, with grim faces, counted the words, shortened the lunch hour and started a system of fines for lateness and other misbehavior. Every day there were new dismissals.

The time of signing in, which used to be the social hour of the day, was now the silent meeting of the condemned waiting for the ax of the executioner ... the dismissal notice that would throw us back into the scrap heap of the unemployed.

Some of us were still too proud to sink back on relief, and we began job hunting. But the mere mention that we had been writers on W.P.A. discredited us for any honest work. It was necessary to make up a story to cover the time spent on W.P.A., and invent fictitious recommendations to get back to the honest, everyday working world.

And then suddenly, out of a clear sky, I found myself in possession of nearly eight hundred dollars. Zalmon Shlomoh, the fish peddler, had died and left me his lodge money and his phonograph with the cabinet of records.

I had moved around so much that the letter from the "Sons of David Lodge" was weeks in coming.

Somehow this death money seemed stranger, more unbelievable, than the first ten thousand dollars from Hollywood. It was just like Zalmon Shlomoh to have paid his lodge dues with the pennies earned selling fish and send this gift to me after his death because I had fled him and his fish smells while he was alive. It was like one of the jokes he made as he wiped his gnarled hands on his sweater, gleaming with the scales of fish.

I saw again the odd twist of his back, and his eyes jesting with me at how own expense. "God sends always to the spinner his flax, to the drinker his wine, and to a Jew his wailing wall." With his Yiddish humor he hid his sorrow and squared himself with fate for his deformity.

Before depositing his check, I looked over his collection of records. Beethoven, Tchaikovsky, Caruso, *Eili, Eili, The Unfinished Symphony*. I played the *Moonlight Sonata*, the one he loved best. Once again, as I recalled the days on the East Side, I was possessed with the old longing to do something with my life before I died.

I wanted to write again with the honesty I knew when I lived on Hester Street. I wanted to make a new start away from the market place where I had lost myself in the stupid struggle for success.

At the public library I came across a pamphlet published by the state of New Hampshire, an open letter addressed to professional people with small incomes.

"Come to New Hampshire! Paint your pictures, compose your music, write your poems. Come, if you seek the peace and quiet of home.... A house and garden for the price of a hall bedroom in the city..."

There were pictures of white houses like jewels set amid green hills and valleys. Among the famous homes featured in the pamphlet was that of Marian Foster, author of *Common Ground*. "Townsmen call her the unofficial first lady of New Hampshire," the pamphlet said. "Her white farmhouse built by her great-grandfather is a place where statesmen, scholars, and artists meet. The world comes to her door."

Often when I had read Marian Foster's magazine stories I had tried to imagine what she was like. Her peaceful tales of small-town folk, *Friendship Village*, had opened to me a new world where people were rooted in the hills and valleys of the countryside around them ... not homeless, hunger-driven, like my ghetto dwellers.

It was the idea of being near her that drew me to Fair Oaks. Because she was the opposite of everything I'd known, I admired her. I thought that for the same reason she would be interested in me and the people I wrote about. I felt I could show her my work and ask her advice.

One spring morning the sky was so blue, the air so charged with hope, that I took the train to New Hampshire. I walked out of the tiny depot that afternoon with the elation of a pioneer adventuring on new ground. The place was not what I had expected from the neat pictures in the pamphlet. Fair Oaks was a wide, wind-swept valley, the earth still brown, the trees just budding. In this vast space a few farmhouses were scattered between mountain roads. There was no main street, only a store, a church, a school, and a gasoline station.

Marian Foster's house stood on a high hill overlooking the village. All the way up the winding path to her door, I was thinking how I would explain my coming out of nowhere to ask her how I could go on with my life.

But when I saw her, she did not seem to think it strange that I had come. People were always coming to her with their problems.

Delight in the world glowed in her eyes. Her graying

ash-blond hair coiled on top of her head gave her face a quaint femininity, a femininity which belied her tailored tweeds and energetic vitality.

I wanted to tell her my real purpose in coming to Fair Oaks. Instead, I showed her the pamphlet with the underlined words? *"A house and garden with a view of the hills for the price of a hall bedroom in the city."*

She looked at the pamphlet and then at me. Her gray eyes summed me up at a glance. She came to the point with the same directness that was in her stories. "How much rent do you pay?"

"Fourteen a month—"

"I know a house and garden you can get for twelve," she said, encouragingly. "Let me show it to you."

As we drove to the house, she turned on me. "No matter how small the amount you have to live on, many around you will be living on much less and enjoying life too."

We came through a garden into a sunny kitchen with an iron sink and a wood-burning stove. The house was empty, but there was a feeling of home about it. Then and there I decided to take it.

I went back to New York to dispose of my things. When I returned to Fair Oaks a month later, I was overwhelmed to find Marian Foster waiting for me at the station.

"How wonderful of you to take time from your work!" I told her.

"People are important," Marian said, helping me with my bundles.

I had expected to live for a week or two at a boardinghouse until I could pick up enough furniture to start housekeeping, but Marian took me straight to the house. As we came through the kitchen door, I saw firewood piled by the stove. Instead of the cold emptiness of an uninhabited house, I found a kitchen ready to be lived in. The stove was lit, dishes were on the shelves, pots and pans in the cupboard.

"God on earth!" I cried. "Who did all this?"

"Your neighbors did it," she said. There was in her voice the elation of having accomplished what she set out to do.

She opened the icebox and showed me milk, eggs, and butter. In the breadbox there was a loaf of fresh homemade bread. Like a child on Christmas morning, I followed her into the living room. It was furnished, even with curtains and a rag rug.

I touched her arm. "How did it all get here?"

"Don't worry how it got here," she scolded. "Just enjoy it."

She went to the door. "I know you want to be left alone to unpack. Maybe you'd like to come for tea tomorrow."

I had always been afraid of the loneliness of the country, and here I was in a strange place, but already I had neighbors, and Marian Foster as a friend. I went to the window to see who my neighbors were, but the nearest house was a whole field away. Lawns, trees, and mountains in the distance were all I could see.

I sank into a wide-armed chair and looked about. This wasn't discarded furniture given like cast-off clothes to the poor. Every piece was still warm with the touch of the people who had used it. They had given what they felt I needed out of their own homes.

Through the window as I sat there, I saw the golden light of sunset on the hills. For hundreds of years the homeless of Europe had dreamed of home. Home in America. And here at last I had found it. This was it. This gift of home.

On my walk along the mountain road to Marian Fos-

ter's house for tea the next day, I remembered Will
Rogers upbraiding me for always harping on the past.
"You've won success the hard way. Must you play the
same tune forever? Suppose you give us another number." That's what I would do. I would learn from Marian
Foster to be happy, learn to enjoy everything and everybody. Instead of the fear and anxiety with which I once
wrote, I would write with joy and thanksgiving.

In my infatuation right after I arrived in Fair Oaks,
I actually believed I could slough off my skin and with
this new home begin a new life. The furniture that was
presented to me, so steeped in the history of the village,
would help me take on the life of the villagers.

"Have you everything you need?" Marian asked as
tea was served.

I told her how much I had enjoyed my first lunch in
the sunny kitchen.

"Only a city person could appreciate the flavor of
fresh, creamy milk and fresh homemade bread—"

"We New Englanders could do with some of your
enthusiasm." She laughed with pleasure.

I looked around her living room. The paneling, the
brasses and pewters around the fireplace shone with the
patina of age and years of polishing. The hand-woven
rug, like the handmade furniture, the lamps, the pictures, reflected the peace of ordered lives. Was that the
secret of Marian's self-assurance?

"Who baked that wonderful bread?" I asked as I
rose to go.

"Mrs. Cobb, who lives in the house next to yours.
She's a farmer's wife who writes poetry...."

"Oh, a poet?"

"It may not be the kind of poetry you're used to. She
couldn't talk about her poetry the way you New Yorkers
would—"

"I'm crazy to know someone like that."

Marian looked at me. Her face did not show what she thought. "I'm afraid it will take you a long time to know these people." She paused and then went on. "If you approach them in the same quiet way they approach a stranger—"

"I don't feel like a stranger—"

"A personal relationship takes time," Marian went on. "It can't be pushed through as you push a button or turn a screw."

I was too excited that first day with my new home, the country air, and the prospect of talking over my work with a writer like Marian Foster to listen to common sense.

On the way back, I saw Mr. and Mrs. Cobb at the window, eating supper.

"Hello!" I called. "Your bread was wonderful!"

She came to the door, wearing a faded cotton house dress. "I bake it every day," she said.

Mr. Cobb nodded to me from the kitchen table. He wore overalls, but even in their cheap, rough clothes, the Cobbs didn't look like farmers. He had the broad forehead, the lean, long features of the intellectual. Hard work and quiet patience were in her face.

"I hear you write poetry. You must show it to me some time—"

She smiled faintly. "You'll see it in the town paper."

"I don't want to bother you," I fumbled apologetically. "But I'm glad we'll be neighbors."

"Well, if there's anything we can do, do let us know," Mrs. Cobb said.

The next day when I went to the general store there were several men in wool jackets talking together in their drawling voices. One of them, a weather-beaten old farmer, was saying, "I turned over the south acre yesterday. I'm going to put oats in there." "Well," another one said, "I tried out that new seed last year, but—"

Their talk trailed off. They were sizing me up.

I walked up to the counter and asked for a box of oatmeal and a can of tomato soup.

"That'll be thirty-three cents," said the grocer, a tall gaunt man. "Seventeen for oatmeal, sixteen for soup."

"Oh!" I exclaimed. "In New York it's only fifteen for oatmeal and twelve for soup."

"This isn't New York," he said.

"Oh, it's all right," I apologized, putting the change in my purse. Their eyes were still on me as I walked out.

That evening as I ate my supper, I began to feel the fear that the country had always roused in me. Living a new life in a new place wasn't what I had thought it would be. It called for a self-confidence that I lacked. I had the old feeling of insecurity, trying so hard to please that I antagonized people.

In the city, for a nickel cup of coffee, or a ten-cent sandwich, I could walk into a cafeteria and see a continually changing current of faces. Some smiled and started talking to you at the counter, across the table. There was a fraternity of aloneness in the city. It was part of the common lot to be alone. But to be alone in a place like Fair Oaks was to be an outsider, a stranger, and separated you from the others.

The next few days I went around to thank the neighbors for their gifts.

"How could you part with that beautiful desk for someone you didn't know?" I asked the plumber's wife.

"When Marian wants anything," she said, "it's always for a good cause. We like to oblige her."

All my neighbors were hard-working women. If they weren't cooking or cleaning when I came in to see them, they were taking care of their vegetable gardens, feeding the chickens, or making their patchwork quilts.

One Sunday afternoon I took a walk past orchards of apples and plums, through a path of blackberry bushes, up stone steps to Mrs. Thompson's white cottage.

The men were on the lawn pitching horseshoes, enjoying a few hours of freedom from farm work. The smell of a New England boiled dinner, pork, cabbage, turnips and onions, came through the open door. Mrs. Thompson, a tall, angular woman in a blue dress and a flowered apron, was bent over a huge wash boiler, cutting soap. She stopped her work to draw up a chair for me.

"Sunday is the one day of rest the Lord gave us," she said, "but if I don't get a head start Sunday for Monday's washing, I could never get done all I have to do—"

"And with all you have to do, you've taken the trouble to send me that wonderful grape jelly!"

Her sun-browned face beamed. "You know what makes my jelly so good? I put a crab apple into my grapes. It makes a finer flavor and always jells."

Hard work and exposure to sun and wind had long ago dried the juices of youth from her cheeks. Her eyes, set deep in their sockets, were the color of the gray ledge in the back of the house.

"I hope you'll excuse the way I look." She pulled off her boots. "I've just come from looking after the chickens. Only half of them are left. Last week a weasel got into the coop and ate up some of our best hens. That cuts down on the eggs, and so I can't have any boughten things for the table."

Pushing a loose wisp of gray hair into the tight knot on top of her head, she went on. "We sure had some hard luck this year. The flood filled the meadow flats full of sand and dirt and ruined our cornfield, but cucumbers and tomatoes we have aplenty. Canning costs nothing but hard work. So I made a batch of piccalilli, sold it down to the store, and that was enough for taxes. There's always a way if you trust in the Lord."

I could only listen to her in silence. Her hardships seemed strange in this picturesque cottage with the hundred-year-old clock ticking reassuringly on the broad mantel, while outside in the distance the hills encircled the place in everlasting security.

I envied Mrs. Thompson her tangible woes, the fact that she could worry about chickens and a cornfield. If I could pin my troubles to something so concrete! I was plagued by doubts and uncertainties, the conflict between what I was and what I wanted to be, the consuming fear that I was nothing, nobody—and the inordinate craving for approval.

Everything that happened to Mrs. Thompson disciplined her faith that whom God loves He chastens. If one thing failed, she knew she could turn her hand to something else. She was anchored in the God of her fathers. But I had abandoned the God of my fathers and had not found my own. And because I was so lost without God, I had such deep need for people.

When I was at the post office one morning, waiting for the mail to be sorted, I heard a voice saying to the postmistress, "I just can't make her out. She's a Jew. I knew that soon's she's spoke. I says to Jim, she's just another one of those writers come to write us up—"

"We're harder'n the rock that goes into our walls. We ain't got souls, she says—" another voice added.

"Well, but I don't call it a mark of brains or soul to go spooking through the hills all hours of the night."

Everywhere I seemed to see suspicion and distrust.

Was it my own fear I saw reflected in their eyes?

Thanksgiving Day I went to see the high-school pageant celebrating the landing of the *Mayflower* Pilgrims. I thought it might help me catch the spirit of the village.

The pageant began with a scene of parting from relatives and friends, heartwrenching good-bys to England. As I watched I felt closer to the Pilgrims, who crossed the ocean in a frail boat, than to their descendants, who merely continued to live in the land made ready for them. The Pilgrims had been dissenters and immigrants like me.

At the final scene of the pageant Marian Foster walked in. She stood still until every eye was on her, waiting for her word. Then she began in her low, rich voice.

"Here we are, all of us together in a spirit of thanksgiving, re-enacting the events of our past."

She knew her audience and they knew her. She spoke to that crowd as if she were talking to each one personally.

"The Pilgrims who founded our country founded it on the Christian traditions of justice and mercy for all. They are not only our physical forefathers, but the spiritual fathers of all who come to our shores, the last comers as well as the first."

She made the familiar words sound new. Her voice was so resonant and had such dramatic control, I felt she might have been an actress as well as the guardian angel of the town.

She ended her speech with "This is our pride, this is the greatness of our country, that each newcomer is given a chance to contribute to the common good."

As we walked out of town hall, Mrs. Cobb turned to me. "Wasn't the pageant wonderful?"

"Well, it was interesting, but I don't see what's so wonderful about ancestor worship." And then I added mischievously, "They say there was only one man among the Pilgrims on the *Mayflower* who could sign his name."

"What does that have to do with it?"

"Of course, it must have taken courage to travel to an unknown country," I said, "but what courage does it take for the descendants to carry on here?" Under her steady gaze, I could feel indignation mounting and I struck out. "I'd like to challenge Marian's words 'Christian traditions of justice and mercy' and tell her what's going on in the world."

"Tell me, why did you come to the pageant?" I had never seen anger under such righteous control. "You come here where every one is minding his own business. Thanksgiving is a sacred day in our lives. We have a just pride in our past and we glory in our traditions. And you from the outside attack us and find fault with us, for doing the very thing that you Jews have been doing for the past six thousand years!"

As I looked at her I saw her anger turn to compassion.

"I didn't mean to hurt you." Humility was in her eyes. "We must learn to forgive people what they are"— she paused—"even before we know what makes them what they are."

The words surged out of her heart to mine from a deeper source than ordinary language. We walked on in silence.

When we reached her house, she stopped and said, "I can't ask you in, because the extra man, who's helping us with the harvest, sleeps in the kitchen. But if you'll wait here a minute, I'd like to give you something for Thanksgiving."

A few minutes later she came out with a package and

handed it to me. Without a word, she walked with me to my house. And still without speaking, we sat down on the log in front of my door. It was one of those rare Indian summer moonlight nights that charged the silence between us with a timeless quality.

Her hand went out to mine.

The river of sorrow that the exiled Jew carries in his heart suddenly threatened to engulf me at her touch, and I blurted, "Tonight I was intolerant—I who suffered from intolerance all my life."

Mrs. Cobb turned to me, her face showing the same warmth that I had seen only for her own.

"I understand," she said. "Our village is slow to take in a stranger. Perhaps you don't realize that you put up a wall around you that shuts people out."

"I do?" the idea shocked me. "I thought it was the village that shut me out. Even you. I wanted to talk to you so many times. I never knew how to approach you."

"I'm glad we met tonight," she said. "There were early mornings when I was on my way to the barn to milk the cows, and I'd see you coming down the hill—so early that you must have walked in the dark—and I wondered about you, but I didn't want to intrude."

"How hard it is for people ever to know each other!" I said.

"You expect too much," she laughed. "You go around looking for perfect understanding, don't you?"

I started to laugh too—the first, free, unself-conscious moment I had enjoyed since coming to Fair Oaks— laughing at myself.

"You see things so clearly. You help me—"

"And you've helped me," she said.

"How could I have helped you?"

"You remind me of all that I once wanted and renounced." She looked toward the hills in the distance, remembering. "When I was young, teaching school here, I thought I was a poet. I had published a few poems and editors had praised them. But I thought I could never try my talent here, in this little town. There wasn't any one with whom to talk about it. Who would understand?

"I had to fight my parents, my friends, and the man I loved. It took courage to go away. And who was I to be sure I was right? Just a teacher in a country grade school. But I had to try it. I had to find out that I was no genius, that love is more important to me than my poetry. And so I came back and got married."

The moonlight animated the lines in her face. I wondered if thirty years before, when she was an eager girl dreaming of poetry, that face had been as beautiful as it was now. Whatever trials she had known she had transformed into tranquillity.

"There were times when I felt half cheated because I know so little of the world outside," she said. "I've been sheltered from the things you know—"

"You know all there is to know about the world," I told her.

She smiled, took my hand and pressed it as she stood up to say good night. "It's taken me all these years to realize that the whole world for me is right here."

Back in my room I opened Mrs. Cobb's package. It was a loaf of fresh-baked bread and a bottle of dandelion wine. Whether it was the release of our talk or drinking that dandelion wine, I slept that night the sound sleep I had not known even as a child. When I woke, my first clear thought was: How could I have been fool enough to imagine just because Marian Foster was everything that I was not, and her writing had everything that mine lacked, that my need for her would rouse in her a responsive need for me, that our differences would be a creative stimulus to each other! Why did I always ask so much of other people, and so little of myself?

It was at Marian's dinner to celebrate the Pulitzer award for her novel, *Common Ground*, that I finally saw the futility of all my attempts to become a Fair Oaks villager.

That night Marian astonished me with her elegance. Her gold-brown velours dress reflected the glints of her ash-blond hair. It was the kind of dress that an artist would have chosen if he were painting her portrait; but she seemed unaware of her appearance. She moved as easily through the room as if she were still wearing her tweeds. As always, I tried to imagine what life must be to one having her ease, her self-assurance. I tried to smile with her smile, but the evil that I knew kept me from her happy innocence.

As from far away, I heard the conversation around me. Walter McCormick, Marian's publisher, a tall, red-haired Irishman with blue eyes, was talking to Marian and her husband.

"'Indian Summer of a Forsyte' is Galsworthy at his best," said Mr. McCormick. "Old Jolyon breaking through the traditions of his generation and the generations before him to touch beauty before he died—"

"Yes, it's a haunting twilight piece," said Mr. Foster. "The solid, acquisitive, middle-class merchant realizing in the end that he can take nothing with him."

"Whenever I read Galsworthy, I remember his definition of art," Marian said brightly. "'Art is the one form of human energy that really works for union and dissolves the barriers between man and man.'"

"I never heard that before," said Mr. McCormick. "It's splendid. I must remember it. By the way, that reminds me, last summer I saw a Little Theater production of *Loyalties*. It's surprising how up to date it still is."

Loyalties! The meaning of the word, the theme of the play, flashed through my mind—what happened to a Jew who tried to get into English society. What would Zalmon Shlomoh say if he could see me here? See to what use I had put his lodge money? I could almost hear his laughter as he regarded me with his sorrowful eyes: "Jew! Jew! Where are you pushing yourself?"

"I'm a Jew!" I blurted.

There was a sudden click of silence. A look of embarrassment closed their faces. After an interminable pause, Mr. McCormick turned to me. "I'm an Irishman, but I don't think it's important to announce it."

After that I neither saw nor heard anything. I got away as quickly as I could. Outside, the cool mountain air washed away my confusion. With a sudden sense of clarity I realized that the battle I thought I was waging against the world had been against myself, against the Jew in me. I remembered my job-hunting, immigrant days. How often when I had sought work in Christian offices had I been tempted to hide my Jewishness—for a job! It was like cutting off part of myself. That was why there was no wholeness, no honesty, in anything I did. That was why I always felt so guilty and so unjustly condemned—an outsider wherever I went.

When I got into the house I began to pack my things. In the midst of my packing, I stopped and wrote a letter to Marian Foster telling her that I was going back to New York.

Her answer came the following day.

I found your note on my desk when I came in from a long stolen day of joy on the mountain! (I should have been laboring at my desk with a thousand letters to do, not to speak of my own work, neglected for weeks, because of such demands from outside.) But my dear husband is going to Wisconsin University to give a series of lectures, and he wanted one last long tramp on our mountains before he left, so I dropped everything and went over to Stratton where he had a Moses-on-Pisgah day of it, with such a grandly spacious view so full of glorious color. I do hope you will soak the color and splendor of the dying year into your heart before you go back to New York.

Do you know that passage from Emerson—one of my favorites—I keep it on my desk: "When a man has got to a certain point of truth in his career, he becomes conscious for-evermore that he must take himself for better, or for worse, as his portion: that what he can get out of his plot of ground by the sweat of his brow is his meat; and though the broad universe is full of good, not a particle can he add to himself but through the toil bestowed on this spot.... It looks to him indeed a little spot, a poor, barren possession, filled with thorns, and a lurking place for adders and apes and wolves. But cultivation will work wonders. It will enlarge to his eye as it is explored. That little nook will swell into a world of light and power and love!"

Isn't this finely Emersonian?

With every friendly good wish,

MARIAN FOSTER.

I reread the letter, stabbed by Marian's cold, clear statement of facts that I had been too muddled to face. She saw at a glance what I had struggled for and failed to achieve, the gap between what I was and what I tried to be—and she could sum it up in a few terse sentences. So "finely Emersonian"!

The last morning at Fair Oaks I woke to the sound of the milk truck going down the road to meet the freight train. I had finished packing the night before. The room, stripped of all of my belongings, looked just as I had seen it the day I moved in. My eyes turned from the rocker to the highboy, to the mirror framed in sea shells. Those prim New England things looked back at me as at an intruding stranger. They belonged. They spoke of stability, security, a homeplace for generations.

I took my bags out on the porch and stood there looking at the picturesque white houses of the valley. It had rained during the night and the freshly washed grass sparkled in the sun. Sunrise lit up the hillside with the last flaming colors of autumn. I watched a farmer ploughing the ground in a near-by field. The place was beautiful, but the sky wasn't my sky, the hills weren't my hills. It was a beauty that pushed me back into my homelessness. I thought of the azalea in its dark, southern soil, banked against the old brick walls in clouds of glorious color; but transplanted from its warm native ground to the cold, rocky New England hills, all its rich loveliness is spent in its struggle to survive as a pale, stunted dwarf.

Mrs. Cobb stepped out on the porch next door and waved. "I may be a few minutes late," she said. "But I put up a lunch for you, and I'll be over in time to take you to the station."

She arrived in an old truck and got out to help me with my bags. Her face was harsh and drawn in the morning light. She looked just as I had seen her the first time I met her, tight-lipped and tired from hard work.

"So you're going back to the city?" The quick little glance from the corner of her eyes, not at me, but in my direction, betrayed how deeply moved she was but embarrassed. Was she sorry to see me go? Was it possible that I had meant something to her?

At the station, waiting for the train, we looked at each other across the gulf of our different experiences.

That searching look unlocked all that had seemed incommunicable between us. The trees, the rocks and hills of New Hampshire, and all the stubborn, unapproachable aloofness in the people of Fair Oaks—I began to understand. I wanted to thank her for turning on her light in my darkness.

"Well—" She started to say something, but the sudden thunder of the approaching train swept us up in the maelstrom of noise. We clasped hands without speaking.

IV

OLD AGE

A Chair in Heaven

I met Sara Rosalsky's daughter, Mrs. Hyman, at the home of a friend where I was baby-sitting. One day she asked me to work for her.

"I need someone to sit with my mother. She is seventy-nine, has nothing to do all day, and she has to have someone to talk to. My brothers don't have time for her, so it's up to me."

Mrs. Hyman hesitated a moment. She gave me a long reflective look before she went on. "You're almost my mother's age, you'd be wonderful company for her, and I'd pay well. I'm a nervous wreck, and I must have a rest. I need someone to sit with her a few times a week. Would you do it?"

She offered to pay five dollars a visit, and I needed those few extra dollars. I agreed to visit her mother Monday and Wednesday afternoons.

Mr. and Mrs. Hyman called for me in their car the next afternoon.

"We'll introduce you as a friend," Mrs. Hyman said on our way to her mother's house. "Mamma loves to talk about herself. All you have to do is listen—"

"But for heaven's sake," Mr. Hyman added apprehensively, "don't let on that you're being paid." He took a ten-dollar bill from his wallet and handed it to me. "This covers today and next Wednesday."

The old lady met us at the door. She gave her daughter a swift, disapproving glance. "Another new suit?" She fingered the cloth of the sleeve appraisingly as her daughter jerked away. "Well, it's good stuff, but the style ain't for you. It makes you look like a barrel of

213

potatoes." Then she saw me. Her gray eyes, oddly young in her deep-wrinkled face, lighted in glad surprise.

"Who is this? Come in! Come in! Don't stand there at the door!" Limping on her cane, one leg stiff with arthritis, she led the way to the living room.

Alongside Sara Rosalsky's tall, wiry figure, Mrs. Hyman looked short and dumpy, over-shadowed by her mother's extraordinary vitality.

"How's my big girl today?" Mr. Hyman kissed his mother-in-law on both cheeks with resounding smacks. Mrs. Hyman retreated into a corner as far away from her mother as possible, took her knitting out of the bag and began clicking her needles.

"This is a friend of ours, a writer," Mr. Hyman waved toward me, proudly. "She heard about your charities for widows and orphans. So she wanted to meet you."

Sara Rosalsky's rapacious gray eyes took swift inventory of the lines in my face, the shabbiness of my hat, the darned patches at the elbows of my sweater. "So you're a writer?" I felt her looking me over with the same intensity with which she had appraised the cloth of her daughter's suit. "If you are really a writer, then I got for you a story! My own story!" She reached for a leather-bound scrapbook and handed it to me. "Read! Read only who I am!"

Yellowed clippings were pasted down with scotch tape. "Sara Rosalsky, President of the United Sisters"... "Sara Rosalsky Donates $5,000"..."Sara Rosalsky"... "Sara Rosalsky." I closed the book and looked at her.

"Now you see who I was! And I'm still not yet dead!" Her voice grew shrill, as if she were still fighting at the pushcarts. "Education I never had. I scrubbed floors, cleaned toilets, and collected garbage from a six-story tenement so my children should have college, so they shouldn't be, God forbid, tailors, janitors, or pushcart peddlers. I made one son a doctor, one a lawyer. And my daughter a schoolteacher—but not an old maid school-teacher. That's why I cry to heaven, after all I did for them why should they leave me so alone?"

Mrs. Hyman's knitting fell to the floor. Her hands were clenched in her lap. "You're not alone now. We brought a friend. And you still complain. What more do you want?"

"How long since you were here? You leave your mother to die alone, like a dog in the street!"

"Shah! Shah!" Mr. Hyman put his arms around Mrs. Rosalsky. "You know Rose thinks the world of you. Why did she bring you her best friend? Come now! Let's have some tea with your wonderful apple strudel. No-body can make apple strudel like you."

He got up from the overstuffed red velvet ottoman on which he had perched precariously, his short legs in hand-stitched gabardine slacks scarcely reaching the floor. Presently he reappeared with a big tray of steam-ing glasses of tea and a plate of apple strudel. The sem-blance of peace was restored.

As I drank my tea, I looked around. Fringes on the window shades, ruffles on the curtains. Shirred chiffon and lace adorned the lamp shades. Peacock feathers formed an arch over the huge gilt clock. All the rococo of the Bronx of fifty years before rioted here, in this room.

I glanced from the figurines and vases on the man-telpiece to the colorful scatter-rugs jostling one another on the red-carpeted floor.

"I see you like my things!" Mrs. Rosalsky nodded, pride of possession shining in her eyes. "I love color, beautiful things make me happy. Those are genuine peacock feathers," pointing with her cane. "And that clock comes from the palace of a Russian prince. It's worth a fortune! I got it at an auction for forty-nine fifty."

She leaned back in her chair, her eyes distantly focused, seeing past triumphs. "Ah-h! When I was young and had my health, I knew how to get bargains!"

"At whose expense, your bargains?" Savagely Mrs. Hyman pushed away her plate and threw open the window, as if choking for air.

Ignoring her daughter, Mrs. Rosalsky refilled my cup, and after insisting that I eat a second helping of strudel, she put the remaining piece in a napkin and smilingly handed it to me. "Here's something for you. Take it home—"

"Oh, no. Thank you—"

"Never mind thanking me, take it. Come soon again and I'll give you more."

As I was being driven home, I said to Mrs. Hyman, "Your mother is so alive for her age—"

"Yes. So alive that she wears us all out." Mrs. Hyman gave a long sigh. "That's why we need you."

The hoarded hurts of a lifetime rankled in her low, tight voice. "Mamma despises me because she neglected me. The days she went bargain-hunting at auction sales, I had to look after my brothers. But if a day passes and she has no one to talk to but the cleaning woman, she phones the neighbors that she's dying, abandoned by her children. She'll never die, she'll outlive us all—"

"No need to get hysterical," her husband laughed. "You know what the doctor said."

Mrs. Hyman turned to me. "She doesn't get under his skin the way she does with me. He can be nice to her."

"It's not everybody can do what she did with nothing," Mr. Hyman said with almost religious conviction.

"In the depression, when millionaires were jumping out of windows, she turned the hard times into a gold mine."

"But how did she do it?" Mrs. Hyman struck out angrily. "Painters, plumbers, carpenters were begging for work. God! How she wheedled and badgered them to rebuild that old rat-trap tenement! Labor and materials, everything—on credit—"

"Sure! She rode over people. She got what she wanted. And that's something not everybody can do. Not every janitress ends up owning five apartment houses."

Mrs. Hyman stared gloomily in front of her. "Just the same, when people say I resemble Mamma, I get frightened. I'd hate to be like her, even with all her money—not that I know how much she has."

Both mother and daughter had left a bad taste in my mouth, and I made up my mind not to take the job. But I had accepted advance payment for my next visit. I decided that it would be my last. However, the following Wednesday afternoon, when I walked in, Sara Rosalsky was so overjoyed to see me that my resolution faltered.

"Are you really here or am I dreaming?" The pleading tone of her voice was like a dog's licking of your hand, panting for affection. "How glad I am to see you! Did you maybe come for more apple strudel?"

"I came because I wanted to see you," I said.

"What a friend! What a pleasure is a friend when alone as I am alone."

She pointed to a red velvet armchair and sat down opposite in her rocker. Her white hair had a natural wave which set off her deeply lined but still handsome face. There was about her an ageless, elemental force hard to define. For a long moment she looked at me in silence. In that silence I saw myself in her eyes.

"Everybody is out to get something. But you're really a friend. You come to see me for myself. Even my own daughter comes only when she wants more money. But one good thing she did yet in her life—she brought you to me. The minute I saw you I felt I could talk myself out to you from under my heart."

The next morning Mrs. Hyman telephoned me. "You made a big hit with Mamma and you did a wonderful job for me. She says you're the only person who understands who she is. She is so proud to have a writer for a friend. Your check for next week is in the mail already."

I needed that check as desperately as Sara Rosalsky needed someone to talk to.

Weeks later, the daughter invited me to dinner. "It's a godsend to have you with Mamma," she said. "I used to be a nervous wreck when I had to see her. Now that she has you to talk to, she lets me alone. And I'm not a bit jealous." She laughed mirthlessly, but jealousy edged her voice as she went on. "I could never figure out Mamma's secret for making money. Even now, old as she is, and without lifting a finger, her real estate is going up. And the richer she gets, the more secretive she is. We know nothing about her will, yet her end might come any day."

But Sara Rosalsky, now that she had someone to talk to, instead of thinking of her end, reverted to her beginnings. "If you only could have seen me when I was young! It burned in me to do something, to work myself up in the world! My aunt who raised me, she hated me. To get away from her I married a man who could not even make a living.... I didn't know I was beautiful till the roomer next door asked to paint my picture. He looked like a prince. And I was afraid... you know men. They don't know when to stop...."

She looked into the mirror. Her fingers caressed her withered cheek. "He said my skin was pure roses.... What a shape I had! Not like the skinny things these days! My bust! My hips!" Her hands rounded out her vanished curves. "And my husband was so jealous when men laid eyes on me! But I know God sees everything And I was pure as an angel."

A smile, a furtive sense of humor glimmered in the corners of her eyes. "My daughter, poor thing, she isn't like me at all. I even had to get her a husband. My son Danny, the doctor, resembles me only in looks. But when it comes to brains, my son the lawyer has it. He's smarter than the others, but smart only for himself. If I'd trust him with my houses, I'd be in the street. God forbid I should have to ask him for a dollar."

Her torrent of emotion never abated. At every visit she bombarded me with another tale of herself. Together with the clippings and photographs in her scrapbook, her words made her seem less and less real, more and more like a record going around and around.... Often, against my will, I would doze off.

Sometimes pride in her achievements gave way to dark memories of her childhood in Poland. "I'd be better off to go begging by strangers than to be a *nebich*—a poor nobody—by my rich aunt. Never once a pair of shoes that fitted me! Everything a hand-me-down!"

The memory was an unbearable one. She opened the scarpbook.

"Look!" she cried exultantly, pointing to a faded photograph. "The United Sisters of the Fordham Temple, at a hundred-dollar-a-plate dinner, in honor of my birthday. Me! I gave it all to charity!" Prominent in the photograph was a huge banner, stretched above the speakers' table: "HAPPY BIRTHDAY! GOD BLESS

OUR PRESIDENT SARA ROSALSKY!"

"Is there a joy on earth like the joy of taking your hand away from your heart to help the poor?" She beamed. "When I sent my birthday present, five thousand dollars, to the Federation, I felt like I bought myself a chair in heaven! And that's when I made my will."

She clasped her hands, gazing at her picture. "Where are they all? They used to come to me from everywhere, like to Mrs. Roosevelt, for my speeches, for my picture in the papers. I was a queen. Everybody smiled up to me. I had a million friends. And now, from all my friends I got only you."

She looked me over with affectionate tolerance.

"If I dressed you up you wouldn't know yourself."

With an effort, she pulled herself up on the cane, limped to the bureau, opened a drawer stuffed with scarves and shawls. She held up one shawl, then another, eyes gleaming. "You never ask for anything. And I like you so much I want to give you something." She wrapped a plaid silk shawl around me. "Why do you dress so plain, like a schoolteacher? This puts color in your face."

I looked in the mirror. The colors were so lovely. "Is it really for me?" I asked.

She felt the shawl with greedy fingers and snatched it off, whisking it into the drawer. "Oh no—this is handmade imported, from France—Paris! But I'll find you something you'll like." She rummaged in her crowded closet and pulled out a faded purple velvet hat with a rhinestone buckle and insisted that I try it on. It was no use attempting to convince her that I could never wear that hat. It was easier to accept than to argue her out of her benevolence. To reassure herself of her generosity, she insisted that I come to lunch the next day.

"You look like you don't eat enough. I'd like to feed you up."

I found the table set as for a feast.

"Is it a holiday?" I asked, surprised at the display.

"Your company is my holiday," she responded gaily. "You make me feel I'm still a person. You know how I can't sleep. But when you come, I forget all my worries and sleep like a child." She leaned over and took my hand in hers. "Tell me, dear friend! How would you like to live here with me?"

I looked at the nightmare around me. The peacock feathers, the gilt clock.

"Why should you pay rent for a hole in the wall when you can stay in my beautiful home and eat by me the best for nothing?" She piled more chicken on my plate. "I love company. If I could finish out my years with you, my friend, always near...."

She had a way of looking at me, seeing only herself. "Did I ever tell you how I started up in real estate with nothing but my two hands?" For the hundredth time she recited her rise from janitress to landlady. "Me, president of the United Sisters! And once I nearly starved to death! Such a story could go into the movies. You could make a fortune from writing my life—"

"Let me think it over," I said, slipping into my coat. She fingered the threadbare elbow of my sleeve. "Here! Let me give you carfare!"

Heretofore when she thought of carfare, she counted out the exact amount of change. Now she pushed a dollar bill into my hand. "Go in good health!"

I left, disgusted with myself for having accepted the dollar. At that moment I could understand the hate that Sara Rosalsky roused in her daughter, so that she had to hire me to substitute for her.

Waiting for the bus to take me home, I watched the branches of the trees against the autumn sky. "Nothing to do but listen," her daughter had said. Good God! The

torture of listening to someone who cannot stop talking!
By the time I got to my room the telephone was ringing.
Mrs. Rosalsky in her imperious voice demanded, "Well,
my good friend? How soon will you move over to me?"

My hand tightened into a fist as she went on. "You
know me. What I want I want when I want it. And I want
you by my side, the sooner the better."

"I'm sorry. No. No. I can't move—"

"Why?" she gasped, shocked into silence for a moment. Then she rushed on. "I can give you everything. I
helped other people. I'd like to help you. I even got a cot
all ready to put into my bedroom. In my beautiful home
you'll have the best for nothing—"

"Thank you, but I have to live my own life in my own
place," I said with finality.

At the usual time I went to get paid. Sara Rosalsky's
daughter lived in a residence hotel on upper Broadway.
Well-groomed people went in and out of the lobby. I
picked up the house phone, asked for Mrs. Hyman. A
moment later I heard her friendly, flustered voice.

"My brothers are here. You're just in time to join us
for coffee and meet the rest of the family."

I was glad of her welcome, but in no mood to be scru-
tinized by her brothers. Though I could not live under
one roof with Sara Rosalsky, I needed the money my
two visits a week brought me. But knowing the daughter and son-in-law was enough. I did not want to get
involved with the rest of the family.

They had finished eating and were sitting around
smoking and drinking coffee when I walked in.

Mrs. Hyman drew up a chair for me. "Here's the
friend that goes to see Mamma." She handed me a dish
of plum pudding. "I knew you were coming, so I saved
some dessert for you."

"And give our friend plenty wine sauce," Mr. Hyman added.

The doctor, a slender, refined edition of his mother, smiled at me. "So you're the lady that Mother has taken such a fancy to?"

The lawyer held out a plump, manicured hand. "Sis has told us about you," he said in a mellow, cultivated voice. "I can easily understand Mother's liking you." Then turning to his sister, "Wasn't it wonderful that we found such a good friend for Mother?" As his appraising glance swept over me, I noticed his short, thickset figure smoothly draped in dark blue, and the fringe of graying hair about his baldness. I recalled his mother's words, "smarter than the others, but smart for himself."

Looking around, I was struck by the contrast between the color and clutter of Sara Rosalsky's overcrowded home and the fashionable austerity of the Hymans' apartment. Here an interior decorator had achieved something bloodless and impersonal. There was a deeper contrast in the faces. The children had their mother's sharp, strong features, but they were only pallid replicas of the mother's extraordinary vitality. The passion of desire which drove Sara Rosalsky had bled out between generations.

To my surprise they knew that their mother wanted me to live with her, and they tried to persuade me to do so.

"Just *like* Mamma to want you all to herself," Mrs. Hyman said. "But in a way it would be a relief if you could do it. The doctor said she may die in her sleep, or drop dead, any day. It would be a godsend for us all if someone like you were there to keep an eye on her all the time—"

"But—" I protested.

"We'd pay you for a full-time job, so you could afford to keep your own little place," Mr. Hyman urged.

I felt the full force of their solicitude mobilized, closing in on me. But I was determined not to be pressed into giving up my entire time to Sara Rosalsky, and so I told them I could only continue the usual two afternoons a week.

It was not until weeks later, when I had stopped in at Mrs. Hyman's for my check, that their real motives emerged.

Mrs. Hyman was serving me tea and cake when she leaned over confidentially. "I feel close enough to you now, after all these months, to be quite frank with you." She smiled nervously, imploring sympathy. "You know how secretive Mamma is. What we've never been able to find out is what she's worth. And yet her end may come any day."

It was all I could do to conceal my embarrassment at what her words implied.

"We all look upon you now not only as Mamma's friend, but as a friend of the family." She pushed her chair closer and clutched my hand with some of her mother's urgency. "You could help us enormously if you could get Mamma to talk to you about her will."

Something in my expression must have communicated itself to her. She suddenly stopped talking. But after a pause, she added desperately, "It's only reasonable! If we knew where we stood, we could plan a little better. Don't you see?"

I saw only too well. But by now I was so deeply implicated, so enmeshed in guilt, that I saw no way out. If I gave up the job suddenly because I hated the hypocrisy of posing as Sara Rosalsky's friend, she would be very much hurt. If I got the courage to tell her the truth, that

I was being paid for every visit she thought to be the visit of a friend, wouldn't that shatter her? But if I remained on the job, I could never do what the daughter was really paying me to do. Now I realized how that first advance payment to pose as a friend had drawn me into Sara Rosalsky's struggle with her children. Anxiety over my involvement grew with my curiosity as to how it would end. With each succeeding visit I found myself caught more and more in a strange double role—employed by the daughter, but wanting to shield the mother from the very thing for which the daughter had hired me.

Mrs. Hyman had always been prompt in mailing the advance payments the times she made no arrangements for me to come to her apartment for a chat. Suddenly, one Monday morning, the check that I had been counting on failed to come. It was inconvenient, but I did not allow it to worry me. But when a week had passed and there was still no check, I was so disturbed that I stopped at Mrs. Hyman's before going to Sara Rosalsky. Over the house phone she sounded harassed and preoccupied. "Oh, it's you? I have your check. I'm on my way down. Please wait there for me."

A few minutes later she came out of the elevator and greeted me with a fixed smile which belied the anxiety in her eyes.

"I've been planning to talk to you," she said, opening her purse and handing me a check. "I might as well tell you right off—it won't be possible to keep you on with Mamma any longer."

I was too startled to say anything.

"You've done Mamma a lot of good. I know she'll miss you. But to carry you any longer is a luxury we can't afford. I've already told Mamma that you've been called to Boston, so she shouldn't pester you with telephones. I'm in a hurry to go to her right now."

I scarcely heard her. I thought only of getting away. I walked the streets hardly knowing where I was going. An hour later, entering the subway, I discovered the check still clenched in my hand.

By the time I got back to my room I had recovered sufficiently to feel vastly relieved. I had been magically freed from an exhausting hell of a job. And I had been paid. I told myself it was for the best.

But as the days passed, I could not get Sara Rosalsky out of my mind. I tried to reason with myself—you were hired, now you're fired, and that's that. But I could not reason myself out of my need to know what was happening to her. She is so alone, a voice within me pleaded. Her children are only waiting for her to die. She has no one but me. I have to go to her. Why so hot on the trail? another voice demanded. What's in it for you? If I abandon her, I abandon myself, my conscience cried.

What had started out as a casual job had become, despite all my resistance, a deeper commitment. You can be fired from a job, but not from a relationship. Yet when I tried to define for myself the relation that existed between Sara Rosalsky and me, I was plunged into a deeper muddle of confusion than on my first visit more than a year before.

I'd wake up in the middle of the night and, in a sudden burst of clarity, hear Sara Rosalsky's voice: "Take a good look at yourself!" As in a dream I saw that Sara Rosalsky was myself, the shadow I had left behind me, the shadow of father, mother, brothers and sisters—the relationships I had uprooted in my search for the life I had never found.

When I went to Sara Rosalsky, after a week's absence, my chief concern was to protect her from the knowledge that my friendship had been hired.

The cleaning woman answered my knock and showed me in. Sara Rosalsky sat in her high-backed chair by the window, staring into space, as if she had lost all contact with her surroundings. The shade was down. Even in the near-darkness I noticed how she had suddenly shrunken. Her nose, her cheekbones stood out sharply. Her eyes were sunk deep in her head.

I glanced quickly at the large, garish portrait of her that I had been called upon many times to admire. The artist had caught something ruthless and indomitable in the young eyes, and in the resolute mouth the fierce obsession of a will to possess—the hunger for love which strives only to conquer. I looked at the face of the dying old woman. Youth, beauty, ambition had come to this.

She mumbled to herself. "With what did I sin? I wanted my children should be smarter than me. College I gave them. Now, my enemies. Why is God punishing me?"

Suddenly she looked up at me.

"Now you come! Now!" she lashed out accusingly. "How could you go away to Boston without telling me? I thought you were my friend, I told you everything! But it didn't touch you! I was talking to a stone." Her outburst gave way to an anguished wail of helplessness.

Peering at me suspiciously, she said, "Did I just talk myself into it that you were my friend?"

Before I could frame my reply, she began fumbling at a tissue-wrapped parcel on the table. "I didn't think you'd come any more. And yet I still hoped. I wanted to give you this." And she thrust at me the shawl with which she had been unable to part a few weeks before.

"There is a God, isn't there?" She fixed the searching sharpness of her eyes on me. "Who makes life? Who makes death? Everything that lives must die. My time has come. I want to die."

She waved a hand at the bottles on the table. "There's enough there to finish me." The ghost of a smile turned into a look of despair. "In God's name! Save me from my children! Please, my friend, help me get into an old people's home! I want to die near people!"

Mrs. Hyman flared up like a maniac when I told her what her mother wanted. "A home for Mamma? She's insane! After all we did for her! Why should a home get the money?" It was as though I had put a match to gunpowder and the resentments of a lifetime exploded. "Senile! Mamma has been senile for the last ten years. Only her terror of dying keeps her alive. She's due for a stroke any day. She keeps going to spite us!"

Early next morning I was roused from sleep by the ringing of the telephone.

"My friend! My only friend! Come!" Sara Rosalsky implored. "Don't wait till I'm dead. They did it. They doped me. They moved me to a hotel where lives my son the doctor."

The door was partly open when I got there. She was in bed, propped on pillows. Her face was gray; sweat gathered in the deep furrows of her forehead. She looked uprooted in the alien hotel room. A terrible sadness was in her eyes. It came from long ago. The unloved, unwanted child persisted to the end—naked, alone, facing death.

She motioned to the nurse at her bedside to leave. I sat down beside her, put my hand on hers.

"Look on the walls! Empty, cold as the grave!" Her voice cracked into a sob. "They tore me away from my things before I'm yet dead—my pictures, my clock, my peacock feathers. I lived with them so long, they were company."

A choking spell seized her. When she regained her breath she dozed off for a few minutes. Suddenly, her bosom began to heave like a bellows. She sat up in a fury of indignation.

"They think they got me in their hands, but even from the grave, I'll show them yet!" She paused for breath, then hurried on. "Nothing I left them! Nothing! Everything I have, more than a million, will go to an old people's home."

Her head sank on the pillow. Anger, resentment, her life-blood ebbed away. In the wide-open eyes, no longer demanding, no longer commanding, I saw the peace that had never been there before. I realized that I was still holding her hand. Little by little, the warmth was receding from her fingers.

The nurse came in, touched her forehead, lifted her wrist. "Dead," she whispered, pulling down the lids over Sara Rosalsky's eyes.

For years after her death, the children fought in the courts for their mother's millions. I could not care who won—the children or the charity with which Sara Rosalsky had hoped to buy for herself a chair in heaven.

A Window Full of Sky

A few blocks away from the roominghouse where I live is an old people's home. "Isle of the Dead," I used to call it. But one day, after a severe attack of neuritis, I took a taxi to that house of doom from which I had fled with uncontrollable aversion for years. Cripples in wheelchairs and old men and women on benches stared into vacancy—joyless and griefless, dead to rapture and despair. With averted eyes I swept past these old people, sunning themselves like the timbers of some unmourned shipwreck.

The hallman pointed out a door marked "Miss Adcock, Admissions." I rapped impatiently. Almost as though someone had been waiting, the door opened, and there was Miss Adcock trimly tailored with not a hair out of place. Just looking at her made me conscious of my shabbiness, my unbrushed hair escaping from under my crumpled hat, the frayed elbows of my old coat. She pulled out a chair near her desk. Even her posture made me acutely aware of my bent old age.

The conflict, days and nights, whether to seek admission to the home or to die alone in my room, choked speech. A thin thread of saliva ran down from the corner of my mouth. I tried to wipe it away with my fingers. Miss Adcock handed me a Kleenex with a smile that helped me start talking.

"I've been old for a long, long time," I began, "but I never felt old before. I think I've come to the end of myself."

"How old are you?"

"Old enough to come here."

"When were you born?"

It's such a long time ago. I don't remember dates."

Miss Adcock looked at me without speaking. After a short pause she resumed her probing.

"Where do you live?"

"I live in a roominghouse. Can anyone be more alone than a roomer in a roominghouse?" I tried to look into her eyes, but she looked through me and somehow above me.

"How do you support yourself?"

"I have a hundred dollars a month, in Social Security."

"You know our minimum rate is $280 a month."

"I've been paying taxes all my life. I understood that my Social Security would be enough to get me in here...."

"It can be processed through Welfare."

I stood up, insulted and injured: "Welfare is charity. Why surrender self-respect to end up on charity?"

"Welfare is government assistance, and government assistance is not charity," Miss Adcock calmly replied. "I would like to explain this more fully when I have more time. But right now I have another appointment. May I come to see you tomorrow?"

I looked at Miss Adcock and it seemed to me that her offer to visit me was the handclasp of a friend. I was hungry for hope. Hope even made me forget my neuritis. I dismissed the thought of a taxi back to the roominghouse. I now had courage to attempt hobbling back with the aid of my cane. I had to pause to get my breath and rest on the stoops here and there, but in a way hope had cured me.

The prospect of Miss Adcock's visit gave me the strength to clean my room. Twenty years ago, when I began to feel the pinch of forced retirement, I had found this top-floor room. It was in need of paint and plumbing repairs. But the afternoon sun that flooded the room and the view across the wide expanse of tenement roofs to the Hudson and the Palisades beyond made me blind to the dirty walls and dilapidated furniture. Year after year the landlord had refused to make any repairs, and so the room grew dingier and more than ever in need of paint.

During my illness I had been too depressed to look at the view. But now I returned to it as one turns back to cherished music or poetry. The sky above the river, my nourishment in solitude, filled the room with such a great sense of space and light that my spirits soared in anticipation of sharing it with Miss Adcock.

When Miss Adcock walked into my room, she exclaimed: "What a nice place you have!" She made me feel that she saw something special in my room that no one else had ever seen. She walked to the window. "What a wonderful view you have here. I wonder if it will be hard for you to adjust to group living—eating, sleeping, and always being with others."

"I can no longer function alone," I told her. "At my age people need people. I know I have a lot to learn, but I am still capable of learning. And I feel the Home is what I need."

As if to dispel my anxiety, she said, "If you feel you can adjust to living with others, then of course the Home is the place for you. We must complete your application and arrange for a medical examination as soon as possible. By the way, wouldn't you like to see the room we have available right now? There are many applicants waiting for it."

"I don't have to see the room," I said in a rush.

She pressed my hand and was gone.

About two weeks later, Miss Adcock telephoned that I had passed the medical examination and the psychiatrist's interview. "And now," she said, "all that is necessary is to establish your eligibility for Welfare."

"Oh, thank you," I mumbled, unable to conceal my fright. "But what do you mean by eligibility? I thought I was eligible. Didn't you say...?"

In her calm voice, she interrupted: "We have our own Welfare man. He comes to the Home every day. I'll send him to see you next Monday morning. As soon as I can receive his report, we can go ahead."

The Welfare man arrived at the appointed time.

"I'm Mr. Rader," he announced. "I am here to find out a few things to complete your application for the Home." The light seemed to go out of the room as he took possession of the chair. He was a thin little man, but puffed up, it seemed to me, with his power to give or withhold "eligibility." He put his attaché case reverently on the table, opened it, and spread out one closely printed sheet. "Everything you say," he cautioned, "will of course be checked by the authorities." He had two fountain pens in his breast pocket, one red and one black. He selected the black one. "How long have you lived here?"

"Twenty years."

"Show me the receipts." He leaned back in his chair and looked around the room with prying eyes. He watched me ruffling through my papers.

"I must have last month's receipt somewhere. But I don't bother with receipts. I pay the rent...they know me," I stammered. I saw him make rapid, decisive notations on his form.

"What are your assets?" he continued.

My lips moved but no words came out.

"Have you any stocks or bonds? Any insurance? Do you have any valuable jewelry?"

I tried to laugh away my panic. "If I had valuable jewelry, would I apply to get into the Home?"

"What are your savings? Let me see your bankbook." I stopped looking for the rent receipts and ransacked the top of my bureau. I handed him the bankbook. "Is that all your savings?" he asked. "Have you any more tucked away somewhere?" He looked intently at me. "This is only for the last few years. You must have had a bank account before this."

"I don't remember."

"You don't remember?"

Guilt and confusion made me feel like a doddering idiot. "I never remember where I put my glasses. And when I go to the store, I have to write a list or I forget what I came to buy."

"Have you any family or friends who can help you?" He glanced at his watch, wound it a little, and lit a cigarette, puffing impatiently. "Have you any professional diplomas? Do you go to a church or synagogue?"

I saw him making quick notes of my answers. His eyes took in every corner of the room and fixed on the telephone. He tapped it accusingly.

"That's quite an expense, isn't it?"

"I know it's a luxury," I said, "but for me it's a necessity."

He leaned forward. "You say you have no friends and no relatives. Who pays for it? Can you afford it?"

"I use some of my savings to pay for it. But I have to have it."

"Why do you have to have it?"

"I do have a few friends," I said impulsively, "but I'm

terribly economical. Usually my friends call me."

I could feel my heart pounding. My "eligibility," my last stand for shelter, was at stake. It was a fight for life.

"Mr. Rader," I demanded, "haven't people on Social Security a burial allowance of $250? I don't want a funeral. I have already donated my body to a hospital for research. I claim the right to use that $250 while I am alive. The telephone keeps me alive."

He stood up and stared out the window. Then he turned to me, his forehead wrinkling: "I never handled a case like this before. I'll have to consult my superiors."

He wrote hastily for a few minutes, then closed the attaché case. "Please don't phone me. The decision rests in the hands of my superiors."

When the door closed, there was neither thought nor feeling left in me. How could Miss Adcock have sent this unseeing, unfeeling creature? But why blame Miss Adcock? Was she responsible for Welfare? She had given me all she had to give.

To calm the waiting time, I decided to visit the Home. The woman in charge took great pride in showing me the spacious reception hall, used on social occasions for the residents. But the room I was to live in was a narrow coffin, with a little light coming from a small window.

"I do not merely sleep in my room," I blurted out. "I have to live in it. How could I live without my things?"

She smiled and told me, "We have plenty of storage room in the house, and I'll assign space for all your things in one of the closets."

"In one of the closets! What earthly good will they do me there?" I suddenly realized that it would be hopeless to go on. Perhaps the coffin-like room and the darkness were part of the preparation I needed.

Back in my own place, the sky burst in upon me from

the window and I was reminded of a long-forgotten passage in *War and Peace*. Napoleon, walking through the battlefield, sees a dying soldier and, holding up the flag of France, declaims: "Do you know, my noble hero, that you have given your life for your country?"

"Please! Please!" the soldier cries. "You are blotting out the sky."

Take Up Your Bed and Walk

For weeks, months, day in and day out, night in and night out, I had wrestled with the tangle of contradictions in my story, "A Window Full of Sky"—whether to die alone in my room in the rooming house or seek help in an old people's home.

By the time the story was published, I no longer cared where or when I would die. Readers sent me letters. I could not answer any of them. Their praises seemed like flowers on a grave, lovingly tendered but powerless to rekindle the spark of life.

Then came a letter that called for an answer:

> In my first year in high school our English class studied one of your short stories in an anthology of literature. I presumed you long dead and was quite pleased to read your recent piece.
>
> I am now at New York Theological Seminary, in charge of the Student Speaker's Bureau. I would like to have you speak to us about growing old in New York.
>
> Our students have a long history of involvement in social problems of our city, although admittedly more often in the area of race and youth, but I think we could all profit from your visit.

The day before I had been hopeless, I could not see well enough to use my typewriter, but this sudden chance to speak to the young was so exciting—I seized pencil and paper and wrote:

My dear young friend,
I was deader than death and your letter called me back to life. Although I'm eighty-nine years old, weighted down with

centuries of fears and worries, I feel myself not fully born. An opportunity to speak to young people about growing old makes me feel there is still something for me to do before I die.

Since I'm not an experienced speaker, I'll begin by reading my story and go on to answer questions.

The date of my talk was arranged, and I was so happy I did not know myself. But soon the old fear and doubt began to shadow my light heart. What a fool I was to grab at the chance to speak when I knew how scared I was to face an audience. Worse than my oncoming blindness was my failing memory. I'd forget a word, or a name; a paralysis of language would block my thoughts.

Distraught, I reached for the phone and called my young friend. But by the time I heard his "Hello" I was too confused to know why I was calling. I managed to stammer, "My magnifying glasses will enable me to read my story. If I only knew the kind of questions they might ask, I wouldn't be so nervous."

"May I come to see you? We could talk it over."

"You mean you want to see me? Thank you! Thank you! Come tomorrow, come any time—" and I hung up without setting a definite time for his coming.

When a few days had passed and he did not come, I told myself he had only been polite; he would not come. Why would he want to see an old has-been whom he thought already dead? The fear in my voice must have driven him away.

I sat at my window, consoling myself with my bit of sky while drinking tea. "When you're old, it's no use wishing for anything else than what happens. He won't come, and I'm glad he's not coming. I no longer exist. Man is but a thing of naught. His day passes away like a shadow...."

The bell rang. I went on sipping tea. Another ring. I

did not want to see anyone. The bell rang louder and longer. I refused to budge.

Before I knew how it happened, Youth appeared in the doorway. Eyes filled with light, eyes that possessed the sky, walked in ahead of him.

"Mrs. Yezierska?" came in a loud voice, leaning toward me as if I were hard of hearing.

He was so radiant I could only gape at him like a deaf-mute, gulping swallows of tea.

To ease his embarrassment and perhaps my own, he asked, "Would you let me have a cup of tea with you?"

I pointed to the sink. Instantly he was there. A cup was washed, a saucepan scoured, filled with water, and on the stove. He found the box of tea, fixed himself a cup, refilled mine, and sat down confidently on the hassock at the foot of my chair.

He drank his tea with such gusto that it made my own taste like wine. I laughed and talked without knowing what I was laughing and talking about. All at once he brought me back to earth.

"Would it be possible for you to speak a week earlier?" he asked. "The man who was to speak on the 23rd of November cancelled. Can you help us out by coming sooner?"

"I-I don't see why not," I stammered, too scared to show my delight. He had seen me—talked to me, and he did not reject me. He wanted me a week earlier!

When the door closed behind him, I walked over to the gas plate and picked up the pot. It looked brighter than it had ever been before. The elan of his youth was still in the air where he had stood. He had scoured the dinginess out of my room and left behind his joy of being alive.

All at once I felt so enriched, so bewitched by the

pure loving-kindness of my young friend that the story
I had planned to read at the seminary—the story of a
frightened old woman begging for a place to die in an
old people's home—was no longer me. I wanted to live
again. I wanted to be born again. But where was there a
place in the world for an old woman to make a new start?

If only I could talk this over with him, I thought.
Hadn't he as much as said to me: "Old woman! Wake up
and live! Take up your bed and walk! You have work to
do before you die!"

The next morning, when the phone rang, I felt him
at the other end of the wire, as if in answer to my need.

"Hello," I quavered in a low voice.

"May I bring my girl to see you?"

I managed to say only, "I would be delighted."

I glanced at the pail of suds and rags by the window.
I wanted to clean my room and dress up in my best.
But before I could do anything, I heard their young
voices outside.

I forgot my crippling neuritis and rushed to open the
door, too excited to care that my old face was still in
my old clothes.

"Come, come in!" I greeted them with outstretched
arms and pointed to the one easy chair in my small room.
"You're the guest of honor—" I told the girl.

"But you're the hostess." With a quick pat she eased
me into the chair and then they alighted on the hassock,
arms around each other, looking up at me as if I were a
person—somebody special.

"Shall we celebrate with a cup of tea?" Jeff asked.

Swifter than lightning they were at the sink. They
were not aware that the gas plate was rusty and caked
with grease, that the battered tea kettle was stained
with soot. Nor did they see the wornout wreck of a

human being whom they had beguiled with the magic of their youth.

"Look at us," I said. "Here we are drinking tea together like a happy family."

I put down my cup and stood up without my cane. "This feast of communication, this flow of soul which you youngsters have steeped into my tea, I'll remember as long as I live."

In spite of their embarrassed smiles, I rushed on. "Your first visit," I told the boy, "Might have been out of curiosity. At best, it was a business visit to settle the date of my talk. But bringing your girl to meet me—" I clutched her arm. "God on earth!" I cried. "With the whole world before you, how did you have time to visit me?"

"Come, come, honey," she said, gently releasing my hand from her arm. "This is the first time Jeff and I had the chance to visit a real live author."

"A chronicler of the Jewish immigrant in America," Jeff added, quoting his high school essay.

As in a dream they had suddenly appeared, and as in a dream I heard myself say, "Ever since I got your invitation, I've been worrying about what part of old age would interest young people."

"Stop worrying," he said. "Anything you tell us about yourself will be great. It seems incredible that an immigrant could come here, not knowing a word of English, and in a few years become a successful writer." His eyes were aglow. "We native Americans haven't the guts to plunge blindly into the unknown and achieve the impossible as you did."

Oi-i weh! I thought ruefully. He admires my do-or-die bravado. A beggar on horseback who drove his horse to death.

"You've been to Hollywood, haven't you?" the girl

broke in. "My grandmother was president of the Theta Sigma Phi sorority the year that you were voted the Most Successful Woman of the Year."

Suddenly their fairytale visit plunged me into the nightmare I had wrestled with the night before, the dream in which I relived the day I faced the Theta Sigma Phi sorority at Ohio State university. Even in my dream I felt the self-importance, the pride born of fear as the applause mounted. There was something to being famous, after all. Success was worth all it cost to achieve. If I were a nobody, they would never have listened to me. But because I had become somebody, I was able to give them something to think about.

I was handed a telegram which I put underneath the others. More congratulations. More good wishes. Another invitation to be the guest of honor at a charity drive. A cocktail party for a celebrity from England. I opened the last telegram casually and glanced at the words, "Mother is dying..."

I do not recall how I took the train to New York, how I found the ward of the Presbyterian hospital. Memory has cut away everything until I was face to face with Mother's dying eyes. Those eyes holding the depths of a soul that I had never before taken time to see.

My earliest dream of becoming a writer flashed before me. My obsession that I must have a room with a door I could shut. To achieve this I left home. And so I cut myself off not only from my family, but from friends, from people. The door that I felt I must shut to become a writer had shut out compassion, feeling for pain and sorrow, love and joy of friends and neighbors. Father, Mother, sisters, brothers became alien to me, and I became an alien to myself.

I was so lost in memories that I was not aware of the silence that had fallen between us.

"You look so thoughtful," the girl's voice came to me from miles away. "Are you thinking of another story you'll write?"

"When you're as old as I am, it takes more time and more labor to get less and less written."

The girl turned smiling to the boy, "Who says you're old? Oscar Wilde said, 'There is no such thing as old age.'"

"Oscar Wilde died at forty," I retorted. "I'm eighty-nine. When I was young, I was the world within myself. Writing was the life of my life. It was my way of being born again."

I paused, afraid to let myself go, fearing that I might drive them away. But once I had started talking, everything in me rushed out to them.

"Last night I could not sleep. I could not rest. And when I read what I had written the last years, I was horrified at the lifelessness of so much labor which ended in nothing. A new generation of writers has risen. They have no more need of me than I had need of the old when I was young."

In the turmoil of emotion that overwhelmed me, my false teeth loosened and threatened to fall out of my mouth. With both fists I pushed them back into place.

They looked at one another, trying not to see me. But in my panic I felt as if my false teeth had exposed the naked skeleton of my dying body.

The girl glanced at her watch. "We really had a lovely time, but we must be going. We've been here most of the afternoon."

"Gevalt!" I implored. "Must you go so soon?"

"We would like to stay longer but we don't want to get you tired," Jeff explained.

"Tired? I've never been more alive," I said. "He who saves but a single life saves humanity. The humanity you saved today was me."

"To be honest with you, we really have to go." The girl patted my hand gently. "I have to turn in a paper by tomorrow morning, and Jeff promised to go over it with me."

"Why...we've just started to be friends," I cried.

"Yes, yes," he said, hurrying her out the door. "But we really must go."

As the door closed behind them, I felt guilt and the pain of the unjustly condemned. A few days later, I received a handsomely wrapped gift box containing eight samples of imported English tea, with a brief note from his girl:

In hopes that others will enjoy tea with you as we did.

The Open Cage

I live in a massive, outmoded apartment house, converted for roomers—a once fashionable residence now swarming with six times as many people as it was built for. Three hundred of us cook our solitary meals on two-burner gas stoves in our dingy furnished rooms. We slide past each other in the narrow hallways on our way to the community bathrooms, or up and down the stairs, without speaking.

But in our rooms, with doors closed, we are never really alone. We are invaded by the sounds of living around us; water gurgling in the sinks of neighboring rooms; the harsh slamming of a door, a shrill voice on the hall telephone, the radio from upstairs colliding with the television set next door. Worse than the racket of the radios are the smells—the smells of cooking mixing with the odors of dusty carpets and the unventilated accumulation left by the roomers who preceded us—these stale layers of smells seep under the closed door. I keep the window open in the coldest weather, to escape the smells.

Sometimes, after a long wait for the bathroom you get inside only to find that the last person left the bathtub dirty. And sometimes the man whose room is right next to the bath and who works nights, gets so angry with the people who wake him up taking their morning baths that he hides the bathtub stopper.

One morning I hurried to take my bath while the tub was still clean—only to find that the stopper was missing. I rushed angrily back to my room and discovered I had locked myself out. The duplicate key was downstairs in the office, and I was still in my bathrobe with a towel around my neck. I closed my eyes like an ostrich, not to be seen by anyone, and started down the stairway.

While getting the key, I found a letter in my mailbox. As soon as I was inside my room, I reached for my glasses on the desk. They weren't there. I searched the desk drawers, the bureau drawers, the shelf by the sink. Finally, in despair, I searched the pockets of my clothes. All at once I realized that I had lost my letter, too.

In that moment of fury I felt like kicking and screaming at my failing memory — the outrage of being old! Old and feeble-minded in a house where the man down the hall revenges himself on his neighbors, where roomer hates roomer because each one hates himself for being trapped in this house that's not a home, but a prison where the soul dies long before the body is dead.

My glance, striking the mirror, fixed in a frightened stare at the absurd old face looking at me. I tore off the eyeshade and saw the narrowing slits where eyes had been. Damn the man who hid the bathtub stopper. Damn them all!

There was a tap at the door and I ignored it. The tapping went on. I kicked open the door at the intruder, but no one was there. I took my ready-made printed sign — Busy, Please do not disturb! — and hung it on the door.

The tapping began again — no, no, no one at the door. It was something stirring in the farthest corner of the molding. I moved toward it. A tiny bird, wings hunched together, fluttered helplessly.

I jumped back at the terrible fear of something alive and wild in my room. My God, I told myself, it's only a little bird! Why am I so scared? With a whirring of wings, the bird landed on the window frame. I wanted to push it out to freedom, but I was too afraid to touch it.

For a moment I couldn't move, but I couldn't bear to be in the same room with that frightened little bird. I rushed out to Sadie Williams.

A few times, when her door was open, I had seen parakeets flying freely about the room. I had often overheard her love-talk to her birds who responded to her like happy children to their mother.

"Mamma loves baby; baby loves mamma; come honey-bunch, come darling tweedle-dee-tweedle-dum! Bonny-boy dearest, come for your bath."

Her room was only a few doors away, and yet she had never invited me in. But now I banged on her door, begging for help.

"Who is it?" she shouted.

"For God's sake!" I cried, "A bird flew into my room, it's stuck by the window, it can't fly out!"

In an instant she had brushed past me into my room.

"Where's the bird?" she demanded.

"My God," I cried, "Where is it? Where is it? It must have flown out."

Sadie moved to the open window. "Poor darling," she said. "It must have fallen out. Why didn't you call me sooner!"

Before I could tell her anything, she was gone. I sat down, hurt by her unfriendliness. The vanished bird left a strange silence in my room. Why was I so terrified of the helpless little thing? I might have given it a drink of water, a few crumbs of bread. I might have known what to do if only I had not lost my glasses, if that brute of a man hadn't hid the bathtub stopper.

A sudden whirring of wings crashed into my thoughts. The bird peered at me from the molding. I fled to Sadie Williams, "Come quick," I begged, "the bird — the bird!"

Sadie burst into my room ahead of me. There it was peering at us from the farthest corner of the molding. "Chickadee, chickadee, dee, dee, dee!" Sadie crooned, cupping her hands toward the bird. "Come, fee, fee, darling! Come, honey." On tiptoes she inched closer, closer, closer, cooing in that same bird-voice — until at last, in one quick, deft movement, she cupped the frightened bird in her hands. "Fee, fee, darling!" Sadie caressed it with a finger, holding it to her large breast. "I'll put you into the guest cage. It's just been cleaned for you."

Without consulting me, she carried the bird to her room. A little cage with fresh water was ready. Shooing away her parakeets, she gently placed the bird on the swing and closed the cage. "Take a little water, fee, fee dear," she coaxed. "I'll get some seed you'll like."

With a nimble leap the bird alighted on the floor of the cage and dipped its tiny beak into the water.

"It drinks! It drinks!" I cried joyfully. "Oh, Sadie, you've saved my baby bird!"

"Shhh!" she admonished, but I went on gratefully. "You're wonderful! Wonderful!"

"Shut up! You're scaring the bird!"

"Forgive me," I implored in a lower voice. "So much has happened to me this morning. And the bird scared me — poor thing! I'll — But I'm not dressed. May I leave my baby with you for a while longer? You know so well how to handle it."

Back in my room, I dressed hurriedly. Why did I never dream that anything so wonderful as this bird would come to me? Is it because I never had a pet as a child that this bird meant so much to me in the loneliness of old age? This morning I did not know of its existence. And now it had become my only kin on earth. I shared its frightened helplessness away from its kind.

Suddenly I felt jealous of Sadie caring for my bird, lest it get fonder of her than of me. But I was afraid to annoy her by coming back too soon. So I set to work to give my room a thorough cleaning to insure a happy home for my bird. I swept the floor, and before I could gather up the sweepings in the dustpan, another shower of loose plaster came raining down. How could I clean up the dinginess, the dirt in the stained walls?

An overwhelming need to be near my bird made me drop my cleaning and go to Sadie. I knocked at the door. There was no answer, so I barged in. Sadie was holding the tiny thing in her cupped hands, breathing into it, moaning anxiously. "Fee, fee, darling!"

Stunned with apprehension I watched her slowly surrendering the bird into the cage.

"What's the matter?" I clutched her arm.

"It won't eat. It only took a sip of water. It's starving, but it's too frightened to eat. We'll have to let it go—"

"It's my bird!" I pleaded. "It came to *me*. I won't let it go—"

"It's dying. Do you want it to die?"

"Why is it dying?" I cried, bewildered.

"It's a wild bird. It has to be free."

I was too stunned to argue.

"Go get your hat and coat, we're going to Riverside Drive."

My bird in her cage, I had no choice but to follow her out into the park. In a grove full of trees, Sadie stopped and rested the cage on a thick bush. As she moved her hand, I grabbed the cage and had it in my arms before either of us knew what I had done.

"It's so small," I pleaded, tightening my arms around the cage. "It'll only get lost again. Who'll take care of it?"

"Don't be a child," she said, coldly. "Birds are smarter

than you." Then in afterthought she added, "You know what you need? You need to buy yourself a parakeet. Afterwards I'll go with you to the pet store and help you pick a bird that'll talk to you and love you."

"A bought bird?" I was shocked. A bird bought to love me? She knew so much about birds and so little about my feelings. "My bird came to me from the sky," I told her. "It came to my window of all the windows of the neighborhood."

Sadie lifted the cage out of my arms and put it back on the bush. "Now, watch and see," she said. She opened the cage door and very gently took the bird out, holding it in her hand and looking down at it.

"You mustn't let it go!" I said, "You mustn't . . ."

She didn't pay any attention to me, just opened her fingers slowly. I wanted to stop her, but instead I watched. For a moment, the little bird stayed where it was, then Sadie said something softly, lovingly, and lifted her hand with the bird on it.

There was a flutter, a spread of wings, and then the sudden strong freedom of a bird returning to its sky.

I cried out, "Look, it's flying!" My frightened baby bird soaring so sure of itself lifted me out of my body. I felt myself flying with it, and I stood there staring, watching it go higher and higher. I lifted my arms, flying with it. I saw it now, not only with sharpened eyesight, but with sharpened senses of love. Even as it vanished into the sky, I rejoiced in its power to go beyond me.

I said aloud, exulting. "It's free."

I looked at Sadie. Whatever I had thought of her, she was the one who had known what the little bird needed. All the other times I had seen her, she had remembered only herself, but with the bird she forgot.

Now, with the empty cage in her hand, she turned to

go back to the apartment house we had left. I followed her. We were leaving the bird behind us, and we were going back into our own cage.

AFTERWORD ABOUT ANZIA YEZIERSKA
by her daughter

Often as a child, competing with the paramount compulsion of my mother's life, and naturally comparing her with "normal" mothers, I had reason to regret that she was first of all a writer.

Yes, it was wonderful to be close to an electric personality who made exciting things happen, who had pulled herself out of the commonplace world, in which I lived with my father and everyone else, and had experienced celebrity, success, even Hollywood glamor. Along with that magic, though, I had to withstand Anzia's emotional tides, the shocks, up-and-down moodiness, exhilaration and depression that constituted her day-to-day relationship with anyone close to her.

Although she had felt compelled by the grim economics and ostracism facing a married woman who chose independence in that time, to leave me with my father after I was four years old, we remained very close. We became co-conspirators, outwitting by our secret understandings the dull routine and promises to my father I had to keep during the six days of the week when I wasn't with her. Her career as a writer began at that point, when she had quit marriage and the duties of motherhood.

A marvel of courage, *chutzpah*, daring, younger in hope and freer from convention than I, she was always, with everyone, centered on herself and her writing; but, because she was direct and unafraid to say what she thought, she could be so magnetic, even to strangers as to inspire unquestioning compliance with her outrageous demands.

Visiting a friend or relative, she might pick up from the coffee table and walk off with a book or magazine, pen and pencils she needed. She collected these involuntary donations without hesitation as her due, because she was dedicated to a holy calling, to which the rest of us should of course pay tribute.

She demanded intensity, instant understanding from others. Exactly as she kept seeking it in her stories, which she rewrote tirelessly, always digging for stronger, more vivid words that would get closer to the bottom layer of her feelings. In the search she might enlist anyone—for example, a girl whose face she liked in the elevator—believing in the ability of native-born Americans to uncover, better than she could in English, the ultimate word that expressed what she really meant. Sometimes she harshly rejected what they offered, when it turned out to be, in her estimation, worthless.

It's hard to recreate the mixed pleasures and pitfalls of being close to Anzia. She combined a powerful intuition, intellectual perceptions beyond her experience, an extraordinary, driving will, and the most child-like egoism and naivete. When she was well launched in her writing career, about 40, (and I was not yet in my teens) she was an auburn-haired broad-featured, radiantly handsome woman, with a white velvet skin, wide, challenging blue eyes, short, broad-hipped, vigorously healthy, dressed always in tailored navy-blue suits. That's her portrait if she ever stood still; but to know her was to be close to an emotional volcano, always ready to erupt.

Since no one, not even Anzia, could sustain for long the intensity she expected, each great experience—the publication of her stories and books, her stays in Hollywood, her meetings with the famous, her loves and friendships—was followed by inevitable disillusionment, which she repeatedly describes in her writing. Even into old age, Anzia, unrestrained by experience, kept picking herself up from these falls.

She was, therefore, the loneliest person I knew. That was part of what drove her to write. In writing, though it required an excruciating search for words that could match her feelings, she found the release and consolation she could not find from people because she demanded too much. She wrote to explain her experiences to herself. Always struck by the wonder of the events in her life, she remained youthful in her reactions to them, as freshly indignant, appreciative, excited as a child might be. That is why the stories she wrote in old age, I think, have the same vigor of emotion, surprise or outrage, as those she wrote in her youth.

But although she wrote about herself, and most of her writing was autobiographical, she was incapable of telling the plain truth. Everything she wrote was fantasy fiction. *Red Ribbon On A White Horse*, which the publisher mistakenly labeled an autobiography, was thoroughly interlarded with invented characters and scenes. And in the days when she was interviewed as a well-selling author whose first two books became movies, a lot of what she told interviewers about herself was a similarly fabricated or at least melodramatized version of her real history. The dates were never accurate. In fact, she knew only the approximate year but not the actual date of her birth and simply invented one for *Who's Who* and other questionnaires. That and the other dates she provided were usually chosen to lop off a few years, for she got a late start as a writer. Her first short story, "The Free Vacation House," was published when she was in her early 30's, her first book five years later.

She emerged as a Sunday supplement celebrity about 1923, perhaps 40 years old, after a movie studio publicity department fed the magazines splashy features about Anzia's overnight rise to Hollywood riches from the sweatshops of the Lower East Side. Whether or not she encouraged this exaggeration, she had a talent for dramatizing and enlarging her life for an appreciative listener. That was probably why book reviewers and interviewers tended to regard her as a "natural"—in other words, a self-educated primitive. They read her books as literally true, in that way underestimating her.

However, I think it is useful to recognize that her need to expand and elaborate on the actual experience was for purposes of emphasis, dramatic effect. The fantasies did not prevent Anzia, as a writer, from exposing unpleasant truths about herself and others. She had in that respect an extraordinary honesty.

Her stories were certainly true to the essence of her immigrant experience, but she often borrowed the experiences of others, injecting them with her own passionate emotions. "The Free Vacation House," for instance, was based on an older sister's "free" vacations in several such houses. This sister evidently had not felt the anger of the story-teller, but she furnished the details to feed Anzia's wrath. *Salome of the Tenements,* her first novel, was the story of Rose Pastor Stokes, a friend of Anzia's from the Lower East Side who also dramatically changed her life—in her case, by marrying an aristocrat of inherited wealth. Anzia omitted her own marriage and motherhood from everything she wrote or said publicly, except for an early attempt, "Rebellion of a Supported Wife," which she left in pencilled notes, incompleted. When she discovered that her road to literature was to write in the Ghetto's ungrammatical idiom, she had to abandon the elegant English she had industriously acquired in night school, extensive reading, and by memorizing the romantic 19th century poets.

I give these examples only because too many com-
mentators on her writing, even in recent years, have
mistaken Anzia's artifice for unvarnished truth. Today,
almost eight years after her death, maybe because the
subjects she chose have become newly meaningful, her
work is being re-discovered by a handful of scholars of
American writing. Two of her seven books—out of
print for decades—have been reprinted in the last three
years and are selling modestly: *Hungry Hearts* and *Bread
Givers*. Biographies and a critical study are in process;
some of her short stories are re-appearing in antho-
logies. And now this present collection. I hope, though,
that modern commentaries will stop repeating the Hollywood myths.

The true story of her life is as moving, I think, as the
manufactured one. I pieced it together from a variety of
documents and memories. She never told it to me in toto.
She was born into a large family in a Russian-Polish
village near Warsaw. An older brother, who reached the
United States ahead of the rest, sent encouraging word
back to the family, and they arrived here by steerage
sometime before 1898, when Anzia was about 15 years
old. The whole family was renamed "Mayer" by the
immigration inspectors, who evidently couldn't decipher,
much less copy, the Polish name. Anzia, dubbed "Hattie
Mayer," didn't retake her own name until she was about
28 and had begun to think of a career—perhaps as a
writer.

She hadn't yet focused on it, because her first goals,
while satisfying certain intellectual aspirations such as
learning English and its poetry, had been to get out of
the Ghetto, escape from the grueling drudgery of the
sweatshops and laundries in which she had buried her

adolescence, quit her Old World parents and lose her heritage as swiftly as possible. She dreamed of marriage and children in the American style, despising the European tradition to which she thought her sisters had succumbed.

She did escape, when she was about 18 or 19, through a four-year scholarship to Columbia University, which she obtained by deceiving some well-intentioned ladies bountiful, patrons of an East Side settlement house, with the promise that she would become a domestic science teacher to help her people, and by inventing for the University a high-school education she didn't have. Disappointed by the dullness of the domestic science curriculum, even in a great American university, she educated herself by voracious reading, especially poetry and philosophy. She had been influenced by her father, a Talmudic scholar from whom she absorbed the poetry of the Bible. While rejecting everything he advocated, she kept looking for God in the literature of mysticism throughout her life.

As soon as she tried schoolteaching, which had once seemed a noble, even intellectual profession, she discovered it to be for her another form of drudgery. Domestic science was far beneath the horizon of her interests. "Who knows how to make a baked ham?" she would ask the students in her cooking class when baked ham was on the lesson sheet; and to the first girl who raised her hand, she turned over the day's lesson.

Marriage also, although she began it with expectation of an ideal, perfect love, turned out to be another form of enslavement. Everyday domesticity oppressed her and, with a baby dependent on her care, she felt locked in a trap for which only the oppressor, her husband, had the key. My father was a schoolteacher and the author of textbooks; *he* expected, along with bliss, a well-kept home and expertly cooked meals. There was a devastating collision of expectations.

Anzia began writing in that period of despair. Her first story "The Free Vacation House" was published. The miracle, the excitement of its publication must have confirmed her in her impulse to escape from her husband, abruptly without warning. She had twice before fled to a sister in California. This time she seems to have intended to return to my father again, but after he retrieved his four-year-old daughter, he said no.

When she did return to New York and tried to get a teacher's job, she was told that she lacked credentials. In characteristic, angry contempt for authority, she stormed without knocking into the Columbia University office of the leading authority on education in the country, John Dewey. He listened to her. She said she had been denied a teaching certificate by ignorant bureaucrats and asked him to watch her teach a class. In such dramas she was a star performer. Dewey actually went downtown to watch her teach, and he read her stories, which she had flung on his desk as evidence of her value.

So quite candidly, he advised her not to waste her time teaching; she was better at writing. Later, he offered her a job as translator on his own research project, a study of a Polish neighborhood in Philadelphia and its political behavior. This was in order to help her pursue a writing career. In fact, he gave her, theoretically for translations, the first typewriter she ever owned. An intense relationship, never consummated, developed rapidly between the seemingly austere Yankee Puritan and Anzia, the passionate rebel. Extraordinarily generous in his understanding, Dewey helped Anzia to believe in herself as a writer and as a remarkable human being.

Perhaps each expected too much of the other. Dewey's poems to Anzia, written in the first flush of their romance, were rescued from a wastebasket by a Dewey student, along with others he wrote, and have been published by Southern Illinois University Press. (*The Poems of John Dewey*, edited by Jo Ann Boydston. 1977) Anzia's story of this aborted love appears, with alterations of names and places, in her novels *All I Could Never Be* (1932) and *Red Ribbon On A White Horse* (1950). She never got over the crushing disappointment. She withdrew from other activities, deprived herself of every social pleasure and, from then on, dedicated herself to writing. Now, to demand attention for her stories, she stormed editors' offices as she had Dewey's, and her work began to appear in magazines, although she remained a poor and struggling unknown.

"The Fat Of The Land," rejected repeatedly by editors, changed her situation. After it was accepted by the brave editor of *Century* Magazine, Edward O'Brien named it "the best short story of 1919," and this persuaded Houghton Mifflin Company to publish a book of her short stories, *Hungry Hearts* in 1920. She sent one of the first copies to John Dewey — to prove herself or to thank him. She sent him succeeding books as they were published, but he never acknowledged them.

One of the fallacies about my mother, written by contemporary scholars who haven't looked beyond the first reference book or catalog, was that she stopped writing as her success waned. Anzia lived to be 85 or 90, and she never stopped writing. Her last novel was published in 1950, when she was 70; her last published story, "Take Up Your Bed and Walk," appeared in the *Chicago Jewish Forum* in 1969, a year before her death.

Between those dates she wrote most of a novel, *The Gilded Poor House*, (which she threw away in a desperate moment), a fair number of short stories and essays, some of which appeared in *Commentary*, *The Reporter*, and *This Week* magazine; a few that remained unpublished at her death, and more than 50 book reviews for *The New York Times*. One of her last stories she left unfinished in the form of a letter to a group of students at Michigan State University. In a course on American writing, these students had read some of her books and were inspired to find out what had happened to her. They telephoned her in New York one night, waking her from a deep sleep at about nine o'clock—for she kept farmers' hours, going to bed when it became dark, and rising before sunrise. They followed this call by writing her letters in which they invited her to come to the University as their guest lecturer.

She was thrilled by this re-discovery, although she was by that time in her 80's and unable to accept the invitation. She started to write them the answer to their questions, the story of what had happened to her. She left several versions and voluminous notes for this letter-story. She was interrupted by misfortune—an operation for cataracts, after which she was forced to walk slowly, with a cane for the first time. She was also compelled to move from New York to a place near me, where she could receive more care. There she returned to the story and began another about the memory-dreams of old age.

As she became almost blind and could no longer read or use her typewriter, she continued writing by dictating to part-time assistants, young students who came after school hours for that purpose. Almost to the end of her life, she was full of wonder and youth, she kept expecting miracles, as she had made them happen all her life.

"Take Up Your Bed And Walk" was, in fact, Anzia's admonition to herself, a final victory over old age and approaching death.

—Louise Levitas Henriksen